CW01669153

A Bible Not Borrowed from the Neighbors.

Essays & Aphorisms on Egoism

Edited by Kevin I. Slaughter

UNDERWORLD AMUSEMENTS

Paperback ISBN: 978-0-9885536-1-3

Collected here are items culled from two primary sources. The first is the entire book *The Philosophy of Egoism* by James L. Walker. Initially my goal was to merely reprint this in a new edition, as it's unavailable but in a rather shoddy facsimile version. Since *Philosophy* by itself is rather slim, and I'd been transcribing essays and quotes to form a second book, combining the two to make a single anthology made more sense, and also would cost less to you than the two works separately. The second source is *The Eagle and the Serpent*, an egoist journal printed in London around the turn of the 19th century. *The Eagle and the Serpent* occasionally reprinted material from the journal *Liberty*.

Another recently published book, highly recommended, is *Enemies of Society: An Anthology of Individualist & Egoist Thought* by Ardent Press. There are two essays that are duplicated between the their book and mine, though I believe that it's such a small repetition that it should not devalue the wealth of material exclusive to either collection for those few who may purchase both.

Efforts have been made to correct any mistakes in the original, and update typographic style.

Footnotes followed by [ed.] were added by me, otherwise they're found in the original text.

—Kevin I. Slaughter
Publisher

Underworld Amusements
Baltimore, MD
UnderworldAmusements.com

CONTENTS

DEFINITION

THE PHILOSOPHY OF EGOISM

QUOTES, APHORISMS, MAXIMS

ESSAYS, EPISTLES, ASSAULTS

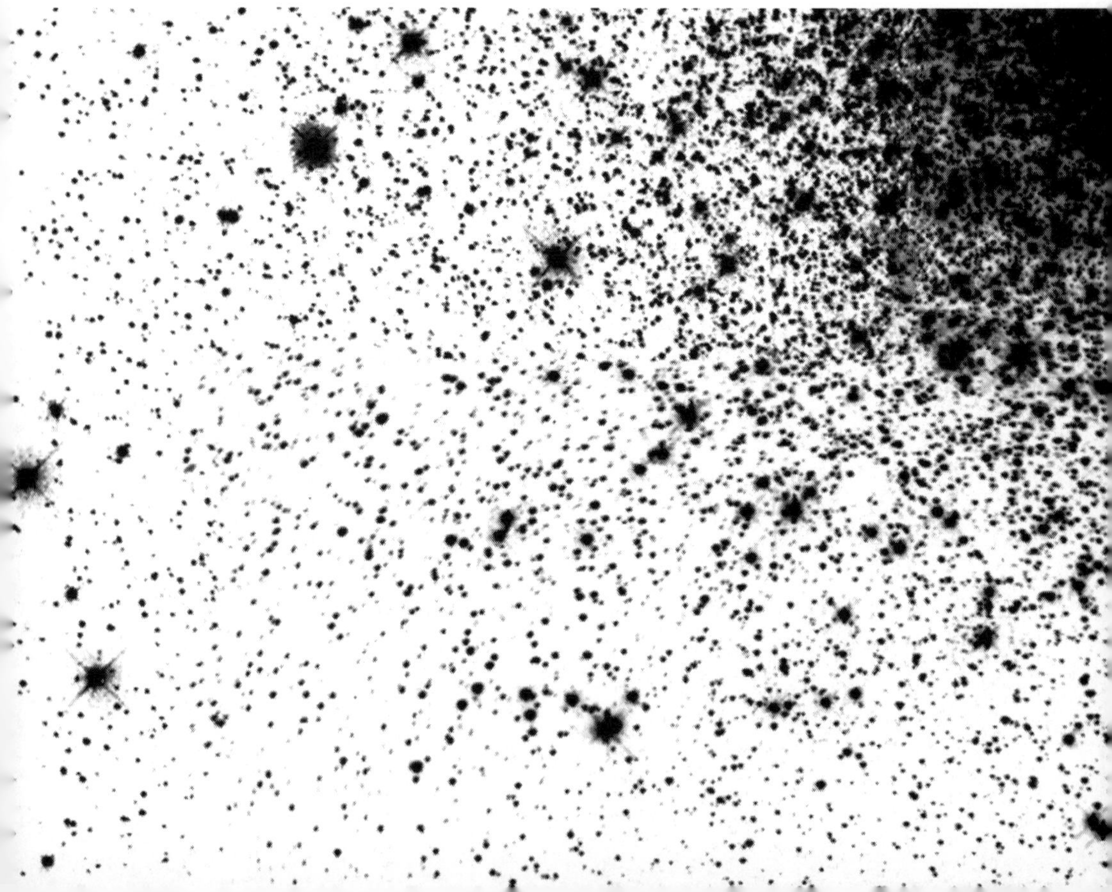

A Bible Not Borrowed from the Neighbors.

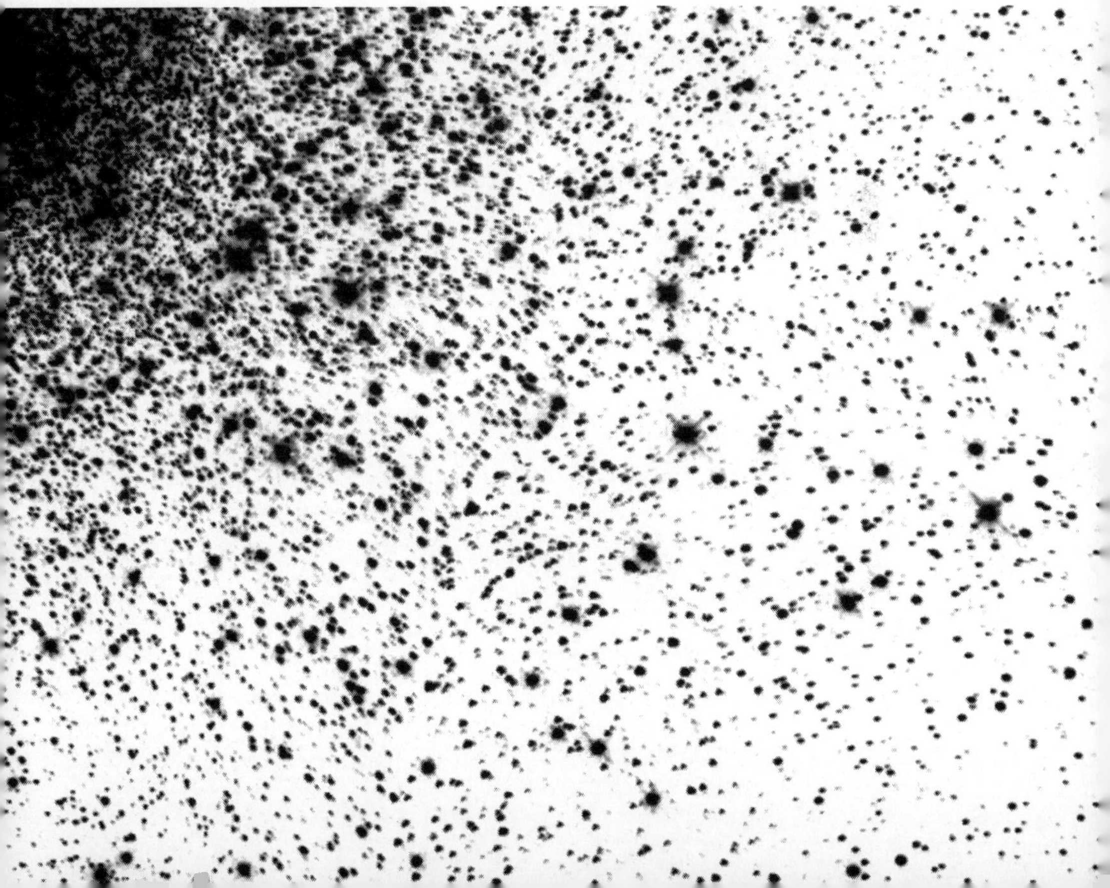

DEFINITIONS OF EGOISM & ALTRUISM

Altruists build in the air. I have unbounded faith in what is called human selfishness. I know no other foundation to build upon. When we cease quarrelling with this indestructible instinct of self-preservation and learn to use it as one of the greatest forces of nature, it will be found to work beneficently for all mankind, and "the stone which has been rejected by the builders will become the chief corner-stone."

—Mrs. E. D. Linton.

The discussion of Egoism v. Altruism in *Liberty* has been very interesting. To me there is no such thing as altruism—that is, the doing of anything wholly for the good of others. We do things for self-satisfaction. I wonder if there are any altruists who would go to hell (presuming there be a hell) in order that their neighbors should go to heaven (presuming there be a heaven)? There is no hope of reward in hell, and a true altruist must expect no reward for his acts. One who would undergo all the tortures of hell so that his neighbors could enjoy all the pleasures of heaven would be an altruist indeed.

—J. A. Labadie.

Egoism is not merely an idea. It is a fact—the force of a man untrammeled by superstition. It may be more or less generous or ungenerous; thus he may be called selfish or unselfish in the common speech. He may be more or less impulsive, more or less deliberate and reflecting. He may so feel and act as to be called very dutiful, the Egoist relation to all objects is conditioned quite differently from that of the mentally unfree .man. If he cares for others it is not because he is taught that it is his "duty"—a teaching which puts a fetter in place of attraction; but it is because he is built that way, and this he knows.

—*Tak Kak.*[*]

ON THE MORAL LITTLENESS OF NON-EGOISTS. In proportion as morality is emotional—i.e., has affinity with art—it will exhibit itself in direct sympathetic feeling and action; and not as the recognition of a rule. Love does not say, "I ought to love"; it loves. Pity does not say, "It is right to be pitiful"; it pities. Justice does not say, "I am bound to be just"; it feels justly. It is only where moral emotion is comparatively weak that the contemplation of a tale or theory mingles with its action, and in accordance with this we think experience, both in literature and- life, has shown that the minds which are preeminently didactic, which insist on a "lesson," and despise everything that will convey a moral, are deficient in sympathetic emotion.

—*George Eliot*

"Duty" never would be missed. The genius performs his benefits for mankind because he is obliged to do so and cannot do otherwise. It is an instinct organically inherent in him which he is obeying. He would suffer if he did not obey its impulse. That the .average masses will benefit by it does not decide the matter for him. Men of genius must find their sole reward in the fact that thinking, acting, originating, they live out their higher qualities and thus become conscious of their originality, to the accompaniment of powerful sensations' of pleasure. There is no other satisfaction for the most sublime genius, as well as the lowest living being swimming in its nourishing fluid, than the sensation, as intensive as possible, of its own Ego.

—*Nordau.*

* Tak Kak was the pen name of James L. Walker. [ed.]

I use the term Egoism, like Stirner for acts of normal self-possession and self-expression, excluding blind crazes, fanaticism, the influence of fixed ideas, hypnotism dominating the subject and rendering him more of an automaton than an individual, although he goes through the motions. Rewards and punishments, promised and threatened, appeal to the Egoism of ignorant believers, but there is also an anti-individualistic craze or fascination in religion, and love and business, when the idea rides the man. In the last analysis it is a question of sanity or insanity. Egoism is sanity. So we use the term, and as Stirner's book, *Der Einzige und sein Eigenthum**, has long been before the world, his admirers have a good possessory title to this term.

—*Tak Kak.*

* There are a number of English translations of the title. Currently the most common is *The Ego and Its Own*, though a different translation used later in this collection is *The Sole One and His Prerogative*. [ed.]

THE PHILOSOPHY OF EGOISM

Prefatory Note[*]

The first chapters of this booklet appeared serially in Egoism, a little magazine published by Georgia and Henry Replogle, at Oakland, California, from 1890 to 1898. It was the intention to run the whole series in the magazine, then publish them in book form; but pressure upon the author's time interrupted his writing, and finally Egoism suspended publication before the articles were completed. Later, time was found to write the concluding chapters, and the Replogles put the whole in type and had matrices made from which to cast the plates, in 1900. But overtaken by adversity and sickness, the matter so lingered that in 1904, when the author, James L. Walker, died, the work had proceeded no further.

A few months after Mr. Walker's death, Katharine Walker, his wife, desiring to have this magnificent monument to her adored husband's memory completed without further delay, undertook the task herself by providing the necessary money, leaving the details of the work to the care of the Replogles. However, the continued illness and final death of Georgia Replogle, and the prostrate condition of Henry Replogle which followed, further delayed the work to this date.

It was one of the ambitions of the Replogles' lives to bring this booklet to the Progressive World with their own hands; especially was this true of Georgia, who, although lying on the bed from which she never arose, yielded with the greatest reluctance to publication of the initial edition by anyone else. In this connection, Mrs. Walker earnestly, but vainly, begged to furnish the means, and keep her own participation in the matter entirely private. But however kindly meant, this was not just

* Original preface. [ed.]

the desired touch; hoping against conditions of palpable despair, Georgia Replogle still hoped in some undefined way to recover her health, and earn by her own hands credit for bringing before the world the first print of this Masterpiece of the Master Philosophy.

The plates of this work are the property of the survivor of this now broken pair of veteran Radicals, and future possible editions will be entirely under his control, as was originally intended of all editions by both of them. So since the fondest hope has been denied by fate, the nearest approximation is maintained by kindlier human effort, in the spirit of Georgia Replogle's most loved passage from the *Rubaiyat of Omar Khayyam of Naishapur*:

> Ah Love! Could you and I with him conspire
> To grasp this sorry Scheme of Things entire,
>   Would not we shatter it to bits—and then
> Re-mould it nearer to the Heart's Desire!

I

We seek understanding of facts for guidance in action, for avoidance of mistake and suffering, and even for resignation to the inevitable. This statement may cover the chief aims of mankind in intellectual discussion, ignoring now that which is merely a scholastic exercise. I am not in favor of argument in the style of the debating school, merely to sharpen the wits. Sincerity is too precious to be tarnished by a practice which easily generates an evil habit, and there are, at least as yet, too many occasions in real life on which every person who loves to tell the truth and expose falsehood must consider time and circumstance lest he impale himself upon implacable prejudices. Consequently if duplicity have its uses there need be no fear that it will not be cultivated without concerted efforts thereto among those who are seeking intellectual light.

I have placed resignation last, though it may be first in importance for some individuals. I take it that the life forces are strong enough in most of my readers to exude in promptings to action which shall move things, in the liberal sympathy which would communicate to others any discoverable means to reach conditions of greater harmony.

Is it not a fact that there is a considerable amount of well wishing and at the same time an intricate series of reciprocal injuries practiced by mankind, such as is not discoverable in any other species on earth? Then, we may ask, what are the causes of evils in society, can they be generalized, and what is the nature or principle of an efficient remedy? If now the words *laissez faire* occur to the reader he will easily remember that all animals except man practise according to that principle. Do we hear of fanaticism among them, of fighting within the species except in defense of their persons and property or on a matter of rivalry between the males? But what do we read in the history of mankind except woes, wars, persecutions and catastrophes beggaring description, and all related in some way to the determination of mankind to interfere with each others' actions, thoughts and feelings for the purpose of making people think better and behave better as conceived?

The theological Liberal is never tired of affirming that the greatest cruelties have been perpetrated by bigots acting sincerely for religious right as they thought they understood it; yet among the theological Liberals may be found prohibitionists and taxationists manifesting a holy horror of a man or woman who simply wants to be let alone while he or she lets others alone, and who refuses to join in any scheme of coercion. They insist that he cannot enjoy such liberty without detriment to society, and their ire rises on thinking that he is insensible to a moral principle, as they view the matter. They are bigots unknowing.

But are there such people as I have alluded to, who practise the rule *laissez faire*? Certainly there are. (These words are French and mean "Let them do," or "Let other people alone as far as you can.") Properly understood and carried out in political science, as by Proudhon, a rational system of Anarchy is evolved from the motto. Anarchy in its strict and proper philosophical sense means "no tyranny,"—the regulation of business altogether by voluntary and mutual contract.

With some readers the perception of these relations as regards religious belief and political institutions and this comparison of human intolerance with the better habit of other species, to mind their own business, will have suggested the fundamental thought to which I am coming. We are digging now for bottom facts; not trying to invent any artificial rule, but to find the wholesome reality in nature if there be any good there for us, and to find the mainspring of normal action at all events, leaving for after discussion if advisable whether or not any artificial substitute be possible or commendable.

Now it is not my purpose to suggest that men should pattern after any other species of animal. We find the other animals acting naturally, seeking their own good, going each his own way and letting each other alone except under certain conditions which have caused a momentary conflict of individual interests. We find human life full of artificiality, perversion and misery, much of which can be directly traced to interference, the worst of this interference having no chance of perpetuation except through a certain belief in its social necessity, which belief arises from or is interlaced with beliefs as to details of conduct, such for example as that the propagation of the human species would not occur in good form unless officially supervised, and so forth. Drawing such comparisons the conclusion appears that man needs to become natural, not in the sense of abandoning the arts and material comforts of life, but in the treatment of individuals of the species by others and in their collective action.

I may here anticipate an objection. Someone will ask whether I pretend that Egoism means the same as *laissez faire*. To this I say no, but the prevalence of Egoism will reduce interference, even by the ignorant, to the dimensions of their more undeniable interest in others' affairs, eliminating every motive of a fanatical character. Invasive developments of Egoism, no longer reinforced by the strength of the multitude under a spell of personal magnetism, will probably not be very hard to deal with; then for want of success such developments will be attenuated or abandoned within the species. Thus Egoism is demonstrably the seed-bed of the policy and habit of general tolerance. And if vigilance be the price of liberty, who will deny that the tendency, within Egoistic limits, to some invasion is the sure creator and sustenance of vigilance? The vaporizing, non-Egoistic philosophers would place tolerance upon a cloud-bank foundation of sentiment and attempt to recompense with fine words of praise the men who can be persuaded to forego an advantage which they might take of others. Like the preachers who picture the pleasure of sin and urge people to refrain from it, their attempts are inevitably futile.

II

It is now time to meet the demand for a definition of Egoism. The dictionaries must be resorted to for explanations of the meanings of most words, but in any science, art or philosophy there are some leading terms understood in a more precise manner than that general notion or mass of nearly related significations given in the dictionary under one term. The dictionary is like a map of the world, which shows where a country is with relation to all other countries. The definition of the dictionary is simply objective, not closely analytical. Its language is popular, as in the speaking of black and white as colors. All this is well enough. People need information which will be true to appearances, for practical purposes, and need so wide an extent of this in a moderate compass, that they are glad to get brief explanations or even hints at meanings, prepared by men skilled in classifying linguistic growths. Hence, however, they sometimes find the popular definitions as good but not better than to define cheese as condensed milk. The so-called synonyms have different shades of meaning, but disputants easily yield to the temptation to assume an identical import in two terms, sometimes for the purpose of blackening one by throwing upon it an evil connotation which adheres to the other; and conversely the hearer is usually able to understand immediately whether the speaker, if sincere, is friendly or hostile toward an object, merely by noting the terms chosen in alluding to its existence. We rarely find many sentences together without a moral judgment being conveyed. Such judgments, from an Egoistic point of view, could be illustrated by representing a beggar extolling charity.

The definition of the specialist, on the other hand, is like a map which shows the boundary between two countries, but does not attempt to show anything else. To the navigator land is that beneath his vessel which is not water. To the political economist a lake and a bed of coal are equally land. The two specialists are concerned with two different series of ideas, therefore with different aspects of the object.

The best that can be said of Webster's dictionary definitions of Egoism, is that a reader who already understands the term as it has been used in practical philosophy for more than forty years, may barely recognize the idea as one espies a diamond in a dust-heap. "The habit of... judging of everything; by its relation to one's interests or importance," is Webster's nearest approach. In what sense can the individual and his interests be other than all important to the individual? Only in the sense that, in order to reject Egoism, his interests are not to be understood as including his intellectual and sentimental interest in objects, including other persons. But the Egoist will take the liberty to inquire how anyone can be engaged in judging of anything without having taken an interest in it. Let us assume that a new dictionary maker inserts in his work a paragraph like this:

> EGOISM, *n.* The principle of self; the doctrine of individuality; self-interest; selfishness.

Then I shall comment by saying that "the doctrine of individuality" is a happier expression than the single word individuality, for the latter is commonly used to convey the idea of distinctive, marked peculiarities of character. Self-interest is usually restricted to pecuniary interest and the like, ignoring what is reciprocal in the pleasures of companionship and what affords intellectual satisfaction. Selfishness is commonly used to indicate self-gratification in disregard of the feelings of others. All these words indicate Egoism, but they indicate it with special determinations. In the word selfish the termination arrests attention. It is generally disparaging; either connected with bad words or it gives them a contemptuous shade of meaning, as knavish, thievish, foolish, mawkish, bookish monkish, popish. Hence when a man acts in certain ways causing disgust in other people they declare his action selfish,—not merely a manifestation of self, but one which they purpose castigating by adding the termination expressive of aversion and contempt. The linguistic instinct appears correct to this extent, however incorrect may be the popular judgment regarding certain actions which are thus stigmatized. For want of this thought some writers have laid the whole popular judgment, expressed in the reproach of selfishness, to the account of opposition to the principle of self. There is certainly a great deal of that. It is selfism of course, which protests, and selfishness which protests most against the selfishness of others and against the principle of self in others. Selfishness argues that its pasture will be greener and richer in proportion as others yield in particular desires to the preaching of unselfishness and self-abnegation, which terms, the genius of selfishness cunningly declares to be synonymous whenever its ends are to be served by such a view. Self-abnegation, however, in its full sense, is evidently insanity, while unselfishness may be only selfism without any feature which can be calculated to arouse the antipathy of other individuals (that is, the un*ish*ness of the self). This is a new analysis and I do not pretend that users of the word unselfish are generally conscious of any force in the termination, to which the privative prefix may apply, but I refer to Webster's definitions of selfishness and self-love respectively for support as to the usage.

III

Egoism is (1) the theory of will as reaction of the self to a motive; (2) every such reaction in fact. This double definition is in accord with the usual latitude due to the imperfection of language, in consequence of which an identical term covers theory, individual fact and mass of facts. I apprehend that in making this fundamental definition I shall have provoked the dissent of some readers well enough grounded in mental philosophy to perceive that on accepting the definition they must speedily consign any claim for an unegoistic philosophy to the realm of mental vagaries. They will accuse me of begging a question in the definition; but I cannot wish to lay down a definition less fundamental than that which will be found sufficiently comprehensive and exact in every relation of rational motive and resulting volition and action. When I shall have done justice to "Altruism" it will be seen that there is here, no begging of any question. The alternatives which the "Altruists" propose may accord with such of their own conceptions as they wish to term "Egoism," with which, however, I have no complicity.

By "the self" I mean the living person or animal, as recognized by the senses and consciousness, and not any mysterious, intangible entity or supposed entity,—"soul," "mind" or "spirit."

By "motive" I mean any influence,—sight, sound, pressure, thought or other energy,—operating upon the self, and thereby causing a change in the self, under which process it reacts to seize what contributes to its satisfaction or to repel or escape from what produces or threatens its discomfort or undesired destruction.

If my definition be imperfect, the gap is in omitting to mention reflex action together with will. I regard reflex action as probably connected with a species of will in the nerve centers (and in other plastic matter in the lowest animals). However this may be, reflex actions are not subject to serious dispute in any speculative moral aspect. The omission, therefore, if any, would concern the exhaustiveness of the definition, not its quality. But the merit of a definition is not in its exhaustiveness; it is in drawing the line at the right place. As I do not purpose further defining "will," I will just say that reflex action being granted to be in effect self-regarding, all that remains to be done in order to universalize, according to these views, the recognition of the Egoistic theory, is to establish all determinations to voluntary activity as reactions, plus consciousness in the brain, like reflex actions without it. Any controversy against the Egoistic theory will rage along the line of voluntary action; hence that part of the line of Egoism is all that is essential to be put into a definition. But if I have omitted reflex action in (1) the theory, I have not ignored it in (2) "such reaction in fact," for "such" refers to the self.

Consulting convenience, I have written "the self" whether meaning apparently the whole coordinated energies of the self or the attracting and repelling powers of any organ or member thereof. Probably never were the whole energies of any animal exerted at once under the stimulus of any motive or combination of motives; hence the common expression is an exaggeration.

A course of reading in history, philosophy and science, especially standard literature on evolution, together with personal observation of animal, including human life, will gradually convince any intelligent person that all voluntary acts, including a certain class of acts popularly but erroneously called nonvoluntary, are caused by motives acting upon the feeling and reason of the Ego, and that the reaction of the Ego to a motive occurs as surely according to the Ego's composition and the motive as does any chemical reaction; that the only difficulty for our understanding is in the complexity of motive influences (motives) and composition of the subject acted upon. To avoid this conclusion the dogmatists have spoken of motive as if it were something self-originating in the thoughts. Plainly, motive is any influence which causes movement. There must be a cause for every thought as well as every sensation. That cause must affect the Ego, and the Ego cannot but react if affected,—therefore according to the character of the motive and the manner and degree in which the Ego is affected in any of its parts, otherwise there would be no nature, no continuity of phenomena. In short, man in everything is within the domain of nature; that is, the regular succession of apparently self-correlating phenomena.

A motive planted in the Ego (that is to say in the self) may be compared to a seed planted in the ground. Assuming that it germinates, the commonly observed effect is an upward growth of stalk and fruit, analogous to voluntary action; but I have defined Egoism by reference to the spring of such action rather than by reference to the action as phenomenon, for a reason which will be understood by following out the analogy. Beside the upward growth there is a formation of root. The stalk of some plants may be repeatedly cut off, but while the root is alive there is the probability of another upward growth. This is most generally the case with young plants. Though mental analysis should reduce will to a mere abstract term of convenience for an imaginary link between motive and act, and whether or not volition becomes differentiated to bear a more precise and active sense, it is necessary to have a conception correlating renewed activities with former ones, as perceived in repetition or in series, without the planting of new seed. This is found not in the simple and familiar illustration of seed lying without germinating for some time, but in the invisible growth beneath the surface, supplying energy and determination to forms which repeatedly appear and then take various directions accordingly as they encounter obstacles.

IV

Beside individuals we encounter groups variously cemented together by controlling ideas; such groups are families, tribes, states and churches. The more nearly a group approaches the condition of being held together by the interest of its members without constraint of one exercised over other members, the more nearly does the group approximate to the character of an Ego, in itself. Observation and reflection show that the group, or collectivity, never yet composed wholly of enlightened individuals joining and adhering in the group through individual accord, has always fallen short of the approximation which is conceivable for the group to the independent Egoistic character. The family, tribe, state and church are all dominated physically or mentally by some individuals therein. These groups, such as they have been known in all history, never could have existed with the disproportionate powers and influence of their members but for prevailing beliefs reducible to ignorance, awe and submission in the mass of the members.

With this explanation and corresponding allowance, the group may be spoken of as approximatively Egoistic in its character. Even when least swayed by individual members, the family, the nation and the church are thoroughly selfy. These composite individualities, as it is the fancy of some writers to consider them, are appealed to in vain to furnish an exception to the Egoistic principle. When Jack imposes upon the ignorance of Jill or upon habits acquired during mutual aid, and Jill is too trusting to trace the transaction back to fundamental elements and calculations of mutual benefit, the matter is readily laid to Jack's selfishness, which of course lauds its victim's welcome compliance; but when the family demands a heavy sacrifice of each member, attention is mostly drawn by Moralists to the advantage of the family and the need of such sacrifices, never to the phenomenon of a ruthless form of Egoism in the family, imposing upon its members who have felt some of the advantages and then yielded to pretensions which will not bear analysis, or tracing back in an actual account of loss and gain. Thus it is said to the man that he needs a wife, to the woman that she need a husband, and to the children that they needed parents and will need obedience from their own children by and by. On the strength of these views various sacrifices of the happiness of man, woman and youth may be effected while they do not inquire precisely what they do need individually and how they can get it at least cost of unhappiness.

The family, attempting to become an Ego, treats its members as an Ego naturally treats available organic or inorganic matter. The supine become raw material. The person has the power to resign self-care and allow himself to be seized upon and worked up as material by any of the other real or would-be Egos that are in quest of nutriment and of bases of operations. The greater would-be Ego, the "social organism," reinforces the family demand with persuasion that hesitates at no fallacy, but first plies the individual with some general logic as to our need of each other, then with flattery, how it will repay him for inconvenience by praise, external and internal, all the while exerting a moral terrorism over every mind weak enough to allow it, and all to subjugate the real Ego to the complex would-be but impossible Ego. For not the good of the family, but of itself, is the object of the state and of the "social organism." The state prates of the sacredness of the family, but treats it with scant courtesy when its own interest conflicts with the family interest. The "social organism" reinforces the family against the individual and the state against the family, this already threatening the family, and obviously it will next threaten the state so far as this can be distinguished from the community; that is the "social organism" will have no permanent use for separate nations.

But in speaking thus we should not forget that the group, or collectivity, reflects the will of some master minds, or at the widest the will of a large number under the influence of certain beliefs. Either one or two or three horses may draw a plow, and its motions will be different. The complexity of motion from three horses is certainly a phenomenon to be studied, but the way is not to disregard the elementary motive forces which form the result by their combination; and so it is with any society. Its phenomena will be according to conditions of information and to circumstances which determine the direction of personal desires. The certainty of desire and aversion as motives, founded in self-preservation, is found in the nature of organic as distinguished from inorganic existence. All desires and dislikes, acting and counter-acting, make the so-called social will,—a more convenient than accurate abstraction. To make of it an entity is a metaphysical fancy. Unity of will is the sign of individuality. The semblance of a social self, apart from individuals, obviously arises from the general concurrence of wills. They could not do otherwise than run along parallel lines of least resistance, but the intellectual prism separates the blended social rays.

The church is an important group, under the theological belief. The primitive character of its dominant idea finds its complementary expression in the simple and transparent Egoism of its immediate motives. A personal ruler, judge and rewarder existing in belief, commands and threatens. The person sacrifices part of his pleasure to propitiate this master because he fears his power. Habits supervene and the investigating spirit is terrorized both by personal belief and the fear of other fear-stricken believers, watchful and intolerant. The hope of heaven and fear of punishment are of the simplest Egoism. Morality on the same plane includes the fear of man and hope of benefit from man, complicated with belief in reciprocal enforcement of ecclesiastical duties, and this as a duty. Becoming metaphysical it is doubtless more difficult of analysis, but this secondary or transition stage of mind is already disposed of as a whole by philosophy, so that the evolutionist predicts the passage of its phenomena and their replacement by positive ideas of processes. The metaphysical stage will pass away though its formulas be entirely neglected by the advancing opposition. In fact, spell-bound and mystified man is freed by courage to break off from the chain of phantasies which has succeeded to the chain of theological fear. In this progress example counts suggestively and even demonstratively, and new habits of positive, specific inquiry give the intellect mastery of itself and of the emotions which had enslaved it.

To sum up this part of the subject, let those who preach anti-Egoistic doctrines in the name of deity, society or collective humanity, tell us of a deity who is not an Egoistic autocrat, or who has worshipers who do not bow down to him because they think it wisest to submit; of a family which sacrifices itself to the individuals and not the individuals' hopes and wishes to itself; of a community or political or social state which departs from the rule of self-defense and self-aggrandizement; of any aggregation, pretending to permanence, that is not for itself and against every individuality that would subtract from its power and influence; of a collective humanity that is not for itself, the collectivity, though it were necessary to discourage and suppress any individual freedom which the collectivity did not think to be well disposed toward the collectivity or at least certain to operate to its ultimate benefit. Self is the thought and aim in all. Selfiness is their common characteristic. Without it they would be elemental matter, unresisting food for other growths.

V

Can the altruistic be included in the Egoistic? According to a standard definition, quoted and adopted in Webster's dictionary, from the *Eclectic Review*, the reply seems to be that it can. That definition reads as follows:

> ALTRUISTIC, *a.* [from Lat. *alter*, other.] Regardful of others; proud of or devoted to others; opposed to egotistic.

If Egoism were the same and as narrow in meaning as egotistic, of course the question would have to be differently answered. But egotism bears the same relation to Egoism as the term selfishness, used with purpose in the derogatory syllable, bears to my newly coined term, selfiness; hence we will set it down that some constructive use for the term altruistic is not of necessity excluded from Egoistic philosophy. But let it be observed that claims made for Altruism, based upon an ignorant or capricious limitation of the meaning of Egoism, and a glorification of the doctrine of devotion to others, intended to produce a habit of self-surrender, are held in our mode of thought to be pernicious, and attributed, in conclusions from our analysis, to defective observations and reasoning, and to the subtle workings of selfishness. To be regardful of others within reason, is intelligent Egoism in the first place, but before we go far in this we draw a distinction between such others as are worth regarding and such others as present no title to regard unless a barren and superstitious form of respect obtrudes itself and makes a claim for "others" because they are "others,"—makes a virtue of sinking self before that which is external to the self. This is the principle of worship, mental slavery, superstition, anti-Egoistic thought. To be proud of others, of the right sort for us, is one form of

Egoistic rejoicing. When reflection has done its work efficiently the habit of care for others, of the right sort for us, continues until checked by some counter experience; but let the habit become strong, let the avenues to esteem be unguarded and the sentiment of worship usurp the place of good sense, then the Ego is undone. He is like the mariner who has set sail and lashed his helm in a fixed position, fallen asleep and drifted into other currents under changing winds.

Some Altruistic writers remind me of the orthodox theologians. In face of the facts of physical science the theologian admits that everything in this world proceeds according to an invariable order, but he insists upon giving it a magical, ghostly origin. The Altruistic writers likewise admit that the immediate choice of action of each individual at each turn in his career is determined by causes with precision, but they plead for an Altruistic education, an Altruistic impulse now, so that hereafter the reaction of the individual to given causes may be this: that he will find his pleasure in the social welfare. I say that if he finds his pleasure in it, he Egoistically promotes it; and if those writers find their pleasure in planning a greater social welfare, their initial efforts in the matter are Egoistic. The reflecting person may perceive that there is room for mistake as to what is the social welfare. The doctrine which demands that a person shall forego some pleasure without having a deliberate conviction that by so doing he makes a wise individual choice, is responsible for a certain immediate lessening of welfare at one point. Beyond that it may be an illusion of ignorance.

The beliefs which prevail at one time regarding what is for the social welfare are widely different from those which succeed them. Once it was deemed injurious to society to teach a slave to read, and consequently injurious to tolerate in a slave holding commonwealth the presence of a free person who ventured to follow his liberal inclination in this respect toward an intelligent slave of deserving character and conduct. Those who yielded to this social belief which they shared, rather than make an exception by following personal inclination, yielded to what has since been generally pronounced to be a malefic error. At the present day the beliefs prevail that conjugal rights of person over person are contributory to the social welfare; that children owe allegiance to their parents, and blood relations peculiar obligations to each other; that citizens need to feel other bonds than their own interested calculations and spontaneous benevolence; and so I might proceed with an array of phantom claimants exacting duties of the individual believer, prescribing what he *shall* and *shall not* do to be a worthy promoter of the social welfare; whereas on the whole there never has been any social welfare understood or realized, but meanwhile trumpery beliefs prevailing in the past and present have filled the world with individual miseries.

Some of the Altruists contend that their ideal man is wiser than to serve the beliefs of society. He works for his own ideal with his own reason for his guide. They fear that if he were to lose the urging sense of duty to the ideal he would cease to labor for a better condition of things. Now this is on their part, when stated, an insidious even if unconscious challenge to us Egoists to show them that Egoism is a better Altruism than Altruism itself. The matter presents itself thus, that the Altruist wants to inquire or discuss whether Egoism is "right," best for society, and so forth. Perhaps it will break up all the societies that now exist, and constitute new moral worlds, making new ideals possible; perhaps liberality of mind will prompt to all and more than the most intelligent and enlightened Altruist expects from the sentiment of duty; but however this may be, we Egoists are not arguing for the right of Egoism to be tried. We are trying to explain that Egoism is the chief fact of organic existence—its universal characteristic.

Let us analyze Altruism with reference to pursuits instead of confining all our attention to persons. A new acquaintance and anew thing are alike objects to the Ego. His aim is to make use of them. The Ego's mental caliber and his predilections, heredity, or habits with regard to association, distinguishing him as an individual, are exhibited in the appreciation which he shows for some objects which can be made use of as means to gain, or reduce to use, further objects. The less reflecting man finds grain and consumes it all, finds wood and uses all kinds alike for fuel. The more reasoning man saves some grain for seed, cultivates it and gets more, saves hard wood for durable uses, makes tools of metal, and studies his future welfare by planning means-to-ends instead of living from hand to mouth. In so far as he, in dealing with either persons or things, keeps in view the rational purpose of becoming better convenienced by any postponement or surrender of immediate pleasure, he is clearly acting with Egoistic judgment. Even when, having tested a series of phenomena, he establishes a rule and allows habits to supervene, saving himself the trouble of constant repetition of verifications, he is still the same Egoist; but if he loses the normal control of his exertions with reference to objects and ends which at first were to him means to other ends, he becomes an idealistic Altruist in the sense in which Altruism is distinguished from Egoism. In other words he becomes irrational, or insane. As some individuals have mind enough to be habitually regardful of others according to their merits, some artisans are habitually careful of their tools and more systematic and steady in their methods of work than others. Does this argue that they are less selfy or does it simply argue that they are more theoretical and, with excellent reason at the foundation, exemplify the law of character by which a process of reasoning having been settled, the intermediate links in some chains of reasoning, become familiar, are passed over without self-consciousness? The selfiness of a farmer who goes out in the cold to save his stock, at the cost to him of some discomfort only, is not less in quantity, but is connected with more intelligence, than that of one who avoids the cold and lets his stock suffer. But a farmer may become so avaricious that he will get his limbs frozen in his craze to save a yearling for the sake of the few dollars it is worth to him. The love of money within reason is conspicuously an Egoistic manifestation, but when the passion gets the man, when money becomes his ideal, his god, we must class him as an Altruist. There is the characteristic of "devotion to another," no matter that that other is neither a person nor the social welfare, nothing but the fascinating golden calf or a row of figures. We Egoists draw the line of distinction between the Egoist and the devotee. It is the same logically when a person becomes bewitched with another of the opposite sex so as to lose judgment and self-control, though this species of fascination is usually curable by experience, while the miser's insanity cannot be reached. The love-sick man or woman has the illusion dispelled by contact with the particular person that caused it; but in certain cases absence or death prevents the remedy from being applied, and in some of these instances the mental malady is lifelong. "Devotion to others," it will be observed, can be made a text for other sermons than those emanating from the amiable Moralists who pride themselves upon the alleged superiority of an unreservedly Altruistic habit of thought.

VI

The man who has fifty or a hundred suits of clothes made for his imagined use, the woman who keeps a colony of cats, the man who fills a private storehouse with all sorts of tools which he can never use, are equally illustrations of the subversion of reason and are to be classed as Altruists in the degree in which Altruism supplants a rational Egoism. Let us take up these cases and consider them in detail. To have more than one suit of clothes is mostly a wise provision for the future, hence the aim is Egoistic, but from the point at which the accumulator loses sight of the end for which his care and trouble are taken, and becomes a slave to the idea of clothes, he ceases to be intellectually his own master; he falls under the domination of a fixed idea and is in that respect like a fanatic. The difference between him and the fanatic is that his crotchet is merely a waste of time and means, whereas the fanatic's fixed idea is one impelling its slave to some sort of senseless interference with other people's conduct. The fanatic, too, is an idealistic Altruist. If his oppression of others were carried on in pursuance of a selfish calculation, he would not be a fanatic.

The woman who keeps an absurd number of cats embodies the exaggeration of the originally rational idea that it is a useful course to have one or two cats about a house to keep the mice down. Care for the useful domestic cat, without reasoning this matter over continually, is just as altruistic and no more so than fair treatment of good neighbors or of neighbors who would probably be dangerous if unfairly treated. The craze for cats is the same kind of Altruism as that which dictates entire self-sacrifice for the imagined good of other people.

One may need many appliances, but there is a rational limit to the accumulation of tools. It is quite clear that some men pass this limit and make collections of such things a hobby, not for exhibition and instruction, because they will eagerly accumulate a dozen or fifty articles of a kind, and not for commerce. This mild form of insanity cannot well be classed otherwise than as a degeneration from rational Egoism, through the altruistic process, to supernal Altruism.

I have dwelt upon these examples partly because it is sometimes assumed that professed Egoists should use neither foresight nor prudential self-denial. Critics who presume to argue in this way refer man to the improvident species of animals and forget even the squirrel. It is quite consistent with Egoistic philosophy and practice that foresight should be used and specific pleasures relinquished, and that habits of prudential self-denial should be formed, subject to searching review and ready self-control, especially as we are admonished on any change of surroundings.

And now, having traced the degeneration of the limited altruistic phase of Egoism (the rational postponement of immediate ends to means of no value in themselves but only to reach Egoistic ends), in other words having viewed Egoism as partly a pursuit of means, and so a rational course, and Egoistically altruistic habits as a further rational economy of time, in place of endless minute examination and calculations of consequences,—having explained from the Egoistic point of view how, when the Ego has in some instance purposely dismissed the immediate gratification of self, he may and does sometimes fail to return to it for want of landmarks, memory and reflection, I would inquire whether there be any better explanation of the origin of the insanity of self-abnegation; I mean in the real, extreme unegoistic sense of the word; a sacrifice without expectation of compensation to the individual. The limited altruistic phase of Egoism is inevitable for a complex being. It involves the peril described. He runs the risk of going into supernal Altruism, much as the sailor, deliberately going out of sight of land to reach other land, runs whatever risk there may be of forgetting the object with which he undertook the voyage or of losing his compass and never getting back; or as an orator, entering upon the flowery path of illustration, may become captivated with the images of his fancy and utterly forget the logical conclusion which he intended only momentarily to postpone in order to reach it with greater effect.

As hobbies, miserly habits, and so forth, do not seem to admit of any other explanation than the one presented, and as fanaticism with its cruel deeds admittedly springs from concern for others, coupled with a belief that certain of their doctrines are errors, and is thus identified despite its deplorable characteristics, as being a pronounced Altruism, and yet in consequence of these characteristics it will not be defended by professed Altruists, but will be admitted by them to originate in unreason, I should not expect them to object to this way of accounting for all obviously evil forms of Altruism. But the obviously evil and the silly phases of Altruism are apparently as intense as those phases which are so much praised and expatiated upon by professed Altruists, and therefore presumably require an equal formative energy. Consequently until the contrary is shown, we shall be as thoroughly warranted in reason in assuming that if the one set have been accounted for by oar theory of the development of the dominating power of ideas and sentiments, the other can be accounted for in the same way; precisely as we may say that if the physical development theory be admitted to account for the snake and the hawk, it will be taken to account for the sheep and the deer. And moreover, when a process of development is shown to hold good, the mute challenge of facts is not merely as to whether or not another and radically different sort of explanation can be supposed for correlative facts, but the presumption of a general unity of process is very strong. Let any considerable part of the foregoing reasoning be admitted and it is granted to us that the concrete good or seemingly good in Altruism is based in Egoism. Then it can safely be inferred that it must be subject to test by reference to the Egoistic reason for its existence; in each case of a development of altruistic motive the question will be: is it serviceable projection, an indirect means of Egoistic attainment, or is it an irrational movement, an aberration, to which we have seen there is a constant tendency?

Now, the reason why we need to speak with caution of the seeming good in Altruism is not founded in any doubt that rationally limited altruism is wise and a necessary part of human Egoism, but in the circumstance that Altruism appears to have been set up by some writers as a principle separate from and independent of Egoism, as if the latter were a preliminary ladder, passing from which they profess to reach their supernal structure, whereupon they would kick the ladder from beneath them. At this point we Egoists decide that such Altruism, considered as a principle, is not a thing of parts more or less good, but is posited as a rival or antagonistic claim, and therefore from the Egoistic point of view, is wholly bad.

Here for illustration we may take the analogy of what is called government. If we say that each individual needs protection from violence and combinations for violence, that therefore the honest people should combine to secure such protection, this is well; but if upon this basis a governmental power is built which proves to be oppressive, we deny that such government is good, whatever good acts it may perform.

VII

All the appetites and passions afford subjects for observation and study of the process traced in several of the preceding paragraphs, but it is not my purpose to give an exhaustive review of the various fixed ideas and fascinations, or forms of mental slavery. I would suggest, as a useful exercise to the student of this philosophy of the actual, that other forms of subserviency to fixed ideas be analyzed as instances present themselves.

Sometimes it will be necessary to look beyond the individual experience of the subject. Indeed it is certain that heredity plays an important part in predisposing the individual to one or other craze, so that he falls into it when the inciting cause arises, or else in organizing him with well-balanced powers so that be happens to be happily proof against their influence. For example it may be interesting to the reader to take up for himself the passion of revenge, study its origin in the facts of warring species, families and individuals, self-defense and precaution, habits of thought becoming fixed, the destructive propensity developed perhaps beyond the need of the individual in actual circumstances, while the sense of relation between means and ends is blunted or lost; consequently when some hurt is experienced or apprehended,—or it may be an insult to his "honor" or a bundle of Altruistic beliefs,—the person seeking self-protection or vindication will act as if what has been destroyed were still to be preserved by annihilating the destroyer, or on a menace he will act with the energy of concentrated race experiences, and in sympathy with his family, nation or race will generalize an injury to someone as being precisely the same as an injury to another or himself, though in the case it may be really otherwise, as a cool judgment might determine. Thus what is primarily self-defense leads, under the influence of this passion, and perhaps quite as often or oftener than philanthropy, to the sacrifice of his own life by the subject. Such action has the mark of that supernal Altruism already abundantly illustrated and clearly distinguished from a rational altruism consonant with the reign of self-interest.

We have now dealt with Altruism as fact, but we have yet to consider it as a preachment of duty. Before entering upon a consideration of the claims of the preachers of "moral duty" and showing what their alleged obligatory Altruism is,—putting it to the test, whereupon I apprehend that it will be found to be easier for a man to pass through a needle's eye than to enter into the moral kingdom of heaven,—I wish to anticipate an objection or criticism which some reader may have raised in his own mind while we were discussing the illustrations of fixed ideas. The miser took pleasure in hoarding gold, but because he was under a fixed idea I classified him as in the bad sense Altruistic; yet for an individual to act under the rule of pleasure is Egoistic. This is the seeming difficulty. It is resolved, of course, by disregarding verbal quibbles. The mesmerized subject seems to act as an individual but he is under foreign control. The miser seems likewise to act as an individual but he is intoxicated or mesmerized by the force of the idea which has obtained an ascendency incompatible with the reign of individual reason.

A further remark seems appropriate here, and I have brought this case up partly to explain how far the philosophy of Egoism differs from the logomachy* of the Moralists, who, not content with dividing men into sheep and goats, would be glad to divide ideas of facts in the same way and on the lines of their own prejudices. With them the facts must be opposites, absolute opposites all the way through, if there be opposition in them in some relation. They have right and wrong, good and evil. Altruism and Egoism in their brains as opposites. Though nothing in fact is simpler to sound reason than the conformity of the crazy

* Logomachy can refer to arguments or controversies over the meaning of words. [ed.]

man's conduct to the order of the sane man's conduct, barring the substitution of an abnormal motive which practically supplants individual reason, the genuine Moralistic theorist does not want an analysis of the facts. He is on the lookout for some peg whereon to hang a charge of inconsistency in argument. Verbiage is his stronghold for such occasions. He may be painfully surprised to learn that we Egoists profess to find the Altruistic subject manifesting Egoistic modes of operation as nearly as the nature of the craze will allow, and that we find in this an expected corroboration of the central fact of organized, sensitive existence. A little shock or whirl of this kind will prepare the less fossilized among my Moralistic readers for the greater astonishment which they must undergo when they for the first time read of right and wrong as they will be treated in these pages, as conceptions having each a separate and independent origin and not logically requiring the usual forced moralistic treatment as if they were necessary and invariable opposites. Just at this point, however, I need only say that modest altruism confesses its foundation and haughty Altruism is self-betrayed, as surely as there is method in madness. Altruism is conspicuously selfish to make gains for Altruism. Method is a prime characteristic of sanity. There may be such madness as shows no method, but it is rare. The Altruism that contains no Egoistic alloy is still more rare if it exists at all. We have yet to look about and see whether it can be found and to examine whether or not it will appear to be a vain profession of self-deluded men who have never contemplated the sacrifices which it would involve if consistently and diligently carried into action.

VIII

To plead before a tribunal is generally understood to be an acknowledgment of its jurisdiction. The intelligent Egoist does not seek to justify his views or conduct according to rules or principles of Moralism which works by awe, aping theology and religion, of which this Moralism is the ghost. Such words as morals, morality, right and wrong, duty and obligation have not lost their limited Egoistic meanings. The theoretical Egoist may be termed a moralist in so far as he thinks out a course of conduct in conformity with his observation and reason. If in a genial way he soars above business calculations then he "sings as the bird sings." To him duties imply persons who have wants and make the non-satisfaction of those wants a source of discomfort to him. But supernal Moralism with its absolute Duty he apprehends as a claim of an essentially religious character fettering with ghostly terror or enthrallment all who yield to the mystic spell.

Persons who have been reared in a religious belief find themselves years after they have become disbelievers in the doctrines taught them in childhood still so far under the influence of religious sentiment that light remarks on the subject give them a shock, and apparently in the same way a generation that does not know God or ecclesiastical authority, a generation that does not know the sacred political State and the sacred authoritative family of its fathers, still retains some portion of the conscience that would fain subjugate Egoistic reason. For thousands of years preachers in the service of rulers have been preaching Duty, humility, submission, piety to the people, and Egoism has been their unspeakable horror. In our day the results of criticism applied to religious belief are apparent in general scepticism regarding the foundation of their authority, of their dogmas. Still the heredity of preaching, exhorting and warning must find its outlet, to say nothing of calculations made by men whose wealth is insured by the system of belief and submission preached, and to say nothing of calculations by ex-preachers of theology whose prospect of an income seems limited to finding something on which to preach and by which to obtain contributions, and thus the relations of man with man, philanthropy for equity, sentiment for science, serve to continue the comedy-tragedy of preaching and servility.

If Shylock does not go to church he takes a magazine and enables the publisher to pay a few dollars a page for essays on ethics, the purport of which is that Morality, Conscience, Duty reign where God formerly reigned and with much the same restraining effect; that all honorable men will agree that these forces are indispensable, ineradicable and necessary for the conservation of property, the family, government and social order, hence a proof of Moral Being in man, while self-interest as a principle would be subversive of Moral sentiment and ruinous to society; wherein it is assumed that society is about as it is desirable to keep it. By such process Shylock makes 5,000 per cent on his investment in Moralistic literature simply in the economic sphere, as he is protected by the State. He accepts any incidental assistance toward keeping women in a receptive and docile condition of mind as being so much clear profit, though really if the enterprise had to be sustained for this purpose alone he must be a miser only or else a free lover and not a "proper family man," if he did not see the advisability of paying out the few dollars even with this sole end in view.

All reformers who are not intelligent Egoists or endowed with the genius of Egoism continually render themselves ridiculous by complaining of monopolists and tyrants. Thereby they proclaim their Moralistic superstition. Their method is abortive. It can at the best lead people from one form of trustful dependence to another. At the worst and often it causes people to commit acts of ill considered hostility and to indulge in sentimental declarations which enable cool and intelligent masters to incite stronger forces against the reformers. Reform, indeed, is a word for conservative mediocrity. Egoism when understood by the many means nothing less than a complete revolution in the relations of mankind, for it is the exercise of the powers of individuals at their pleasure, and not a plea for their "rights."

The Moralists, or Altruists, come with a tale of Duty, or moral obligation. They say that I ought to love my neighbor as myself and to put aside my selfy pleasure. It is horrifying to them that I act on consciousness of satisfaction, on genial impulse, on calculation of gain, and not in submission to the Moralistic judgment of "conscience." I understand very well that it is their ignorant fear of an independent person that is at the bottom of their pleading. They are accustomed to think of a man as a dangerous animal unless controlled by "conscience." Few of them have met one who does not profess to defer to such a "spiritual guide." I however regard their "conscience" as identical with the superstition which impels Hindus to throw themselves beneath the wheels of the sacred car and to allow sacred animals and sacred men to devour their substance.

Are the Altruists, the Moralists, willing to examine the logic of their principle and carry it out to its consequences? Will they follow where it leads? Then we need not insist upon the prominence of the oppressive idea of Duty and its degradation of the individual, but we may take their own favorite idea of pure, disinterested love expelling self-interest whereever the two conflict. Of course the intelligent Egoist will perceive that I am trying to accommodate the Altruists, to get as near their position as possible, but that nevertheless there is something of falsehood, of contradiction, in the idea that love can be other than a personal interest in the object when love overcomes other interests without a sentiment of sacrifice arising; and that if the consciousness of sacrifice be present the motive is Duty, not love. However, I am discussing an alleged possibility,—a life of Altruistic devotion,—and I do not expect in the statement of the question to succeed better than the Moralists themselves in making the fanciful scheme appear wholly real.

Apart from theology with its gross dogmatism about "souls" in men and the animals as "soulless" machines of flesh and blood, the dogma of Moralism, the duty of love to others, obviously bears a direct and essential relation to the capacity of others to enjoy and to suffer, and no radical distinction can be made between a human subject and any other animal. The anti-vivisection Moralists stand up to the logic of their principle in one particular when they insist that pain ought not to be inflicted upon the inferior animals for the advancement of science intended for the benefit of mankind and not for the species or individual animals operated upon.

The consistent Moralist will now see what his principle requires of him. Though the animal, by reason of its inferior intelligence and want of speech and hands, cannot fully express its complaints, assert its "rights," and maintain its liberty, he will neither use his superior ability to enslave it nor permit others to do such wrong if it be within his power to prevent them. The animal's inability to participate as an equal in social affairs is ground for certain exclusions, but not for usurpation, detention, subjugation, castration, enforced labor, shearing off the natural coat, robbery of the mother's milk and driving to the slaughter house. By what right does the Moralist shoot deer or crows, cut off the heads of chickens and turkeys, and cast his line or his net for fish? If by the authority of God, I reply that God is the archetype of personal despotism,—Egoism without the balancing force of approximately equal powers in different individuals; and that there is no such authority. The philosophical Altruist has left that ground. I refuse to recognize the plea. I look to the Altruistic Moralist for a less barbarian answer. And let him remember the incapable of his species,—the idiot, the maniac. Does he exploit them with a good conscience, as he tames and rides a horse? Does he refrain from fattening and killing them only because he thinks they are not good eating? Where and what is his conscience, then, as to other animals?

Permit me to suggest that a man is safe in reflecting that he will never be a buffalo or a rat,—unless he believes in transmigration, whereupon his unconfessed Egoism crops out, keenly self-regardful. Hence buffaloes and rats have no rights that a man even though a professed Moralist need respect, except the right of exemption from torture. (Torture is a bad example. It can be inflicted upon men as well as upon other animals and it does not minister to any demand of enlightened self-interest.) But what man may not be accused of feeblemindedness or suffer some accident which will impair his mental powers? How then can self-concern be silent when one of his species is ill treated? The other animals—indeed he is never to be one of them: what does it matter to him how you use them so that you do not cultivate cruelty in yourself? (The cruel man is dangerous to us and ours.)

I call upon the Moralist to vindicate his doctrine by applying it consistently to the treatment of all animals. Confining it to our own species is too Egoistic to be deemed pure Moralism. I shall be very much surprised if any such practical response comes as to disprove my new version of scripture, which says that the Moral kingdom of heaven is inaccessible to men of ordinary sanity. Who will rejoice to see the grasshopper getting his fill, and keep sacrilegious hands out of the hen's nest? Who will feed the lambs and neither feed upon lamb nor wrap in woolen blankets, for conscience sake? One Moralist has one hobby and another has another hobby, but if there be one who proposes to live a life of self-denial for the happiness of all other sentient beings as far as they are capable of experiencing pleasure, to respect their liberty and embryonic offspring as conscientiously as any Moralist does those of his own species, I shall regard his appearance upon this scene as the exception which will very strikingly illustrate the rule in individual conduct, and I shall be glad to have an opportunity of learning how he manages to live.

IX

If self-renunciation be a virtue, certainly it is the purer when the sacrifice is made for individuals of another and widely different species. In caring for our own species we may obtain a return, and we can cherish the imagination thereof if it seems improbable; and so it is in caring for one of any other species between which and ourselves there is some communication of mutual intelligence and mutual sympathy; but if a man wants to show pure disinterestedness let him sacrifice his pleasure, his comfort and his life for other species that will neither understand nor return the manifestation of benevolence. Such a supernal Altruist will reject cleanliness as a sin, if convinced, as he must be by ordinary observation, that parasites thrive best on the human body when there is an entire avoidance of soap and water. Such a self-denying Moralist will not dress a wound or purify his blood, for these practices mean death to animalcules*. Here I am reminded of the story of the devout Hindu who was horrified on looking at a drop of water through a powerful microscope. He found to his consternation that he could not drink without destroying life.

Supernal Moralism should be viewed sometimes from the point of view of universal animal motives and conduct, excluding the idea of selflessness. If the survival of the fittest be not an empty phrase, supernal Moralism is an excessively silly insanity. The "sacredness" of the germs of human life is impressed upon the mind of the devotee of Moralism, and in some cases the result is that a child is born as the offspring of rape. The simple, pious people may wonder that "God" can assist in giving effect to crime. The supernal Moralist who prides himself on scientific acquirements may well feel confused when a hybrid form appears as a practical commentary upon the alleged "sacredness."

* "Animalculs" is an archaic term for microscopic animals. [ed.]

Spiritual terror, the strangest, most melancholy phenomenon in human motive, is essentially the same influence, while it lasts, in the man or woman claiming to be emancipated from theological dogmas, as in the believer in those dogmas. It usually remains after its generally supposed root is destroyed, in the Agnostic, like an air-plant. This indicates that its foundation is not precisely where some anti-theological writers suppose. Mere disbelief in Jehovah may leave the agnostic mind subject to fixed ideas of a most irrational character. The belief in Jehovah in the first place occupied an ignorant mind and when that belief is expelled neither ignorance nor fear is altogether banished. There is some improvement in the prospect for positive Egoistic thought and sentiment to occupy its own. There remain, however, numerous fixed ideas of Duty to Society, Duty to the State, Duty to Humanity, and such rubbish, which are fertile of intoxicating and paralyzing influences, and our talking Freethinkers in general still shudder to contemplate a person uncontrolled by such "restraining influences." They imagine, after all, that he will go to the devil or run amuck without moral "restraint." The triumph of sanity, then, lies not in the expulsion of any one form of insanity, but in the acquisition of an Egoistic consciousness and self-control.

X

Under the head of Religion Webster's dictionary says: "As distinguished from morality, religion denotes the influences and motives to human duty which are found in the character and will of God, while morality describes the duties to man, to which true religion always influences." Granted belief in a personal ruler, submission to his will is prudence, and prudence is Egoistic. With this conception the duty spoken of is not mysterious: it is service by a subject,—the slave's submission to the power which he fears. He believes that the sovereign ruler has laid upon him special commands favoring his species and therefore he must treat men better than other animals. If this belief be an error, still there is no line to be drawn between the alleged duty and his interest. There is no disinterestedness or generosity in religious duty or moral duty,—or say rather in duty to God or man, for both are ultimately duty to the supposed heavenly' master.

But Moralists, having gained some rational ideas of mutual relations, while unhappily ignoring the fact that these ideas are the proper foundation of willingly assumed mutual duties, fancy that they have discovered the justice of the alleged divine command or will, which is nothing but a reflection of their own thoughts, and thenceforth they fall under the hallucination of mystic Duty, independent of either calculation or pleasure. It is one task of Egoistic philosophy to analyze this notion of theirs as a confusion of ideas. They go so far in some instances as to dismiss belief in a moral lawgiver of the universe and yet remain under the same fascination to Duty as if they had him, and his will were equitable, and their servility were swallowed up in admiration of his justice. What they lack is the insight to perceive that conduct which makes for the good of the species is naturally agreeable to the feeling of each well developed Individual, hence that the conception of Duty is scepticism as to spontaneity. The fixed idea of Duty unrelated to interest and not reducible to calculation, arises by abstraction and fascination like other aberrations reviewed in preceding pages. It reaches clear insanity in self-sacrifice if this occur in unreasoning ecstacy.

Of course one self-inflicted pain of some particular kind or even death is sometimes chosen in order to terminate anguish which none but the subject can appreciate. In such cases the action is Egoistic, though it may be of a terribly ignorant sort, as for example, when the cause of the pain is an imaginary object or such a real relation as is humiliating to the person's feeling only because of irrational notions about it.

If morality be regarded from the point of view of the social utilitarian, as that course of conduct which promotes the welfare of the species, it is only necessary to repeat that the species acts as Egoistically as it can. It cheerfully sacrifices individuals to its own welfare. It has a subtle economy of means in planting Altruistic conceits in those that are willing to entertain them. When intelligence comes to recognize mutual interest this instinctive trickery of social influence will vanish, no longer seeming to be needed.

As for the virtues, such as benevolence, every observing person knows that we seek to get rid of painful impressions. Such, usually, are those of suffering in others. Many writers have pointed out how pity is stirred by the sight of wasted bodies and hearing the cry of pain, and how much weaker it is when only an ordinary description is given of the occasion; also how much more ready the poor are to help other poor people than the rich are. What has perhaps not been so generally observed is the reason for this, *viz.*,* that the rich do not feel that they are likely to need alms, while the poor are on the edge of such need. There is quite enough in the difference of circumstances to make it

* *Viz.* is a typographic shorthand for the Latin *vidēre licet*, which meant "it may be seen, evidently, clearly." [ed.]

instructive, although at the same time, personal character varying in susceptibility, it is doubt, less true also that those most inclined to benevolence are most likely to be poor in a society like ours, where money is supposed to grow by lending and profits are consolidated from the results of unpaid labor.

XI

The suggestion has been heard that if all acts are Egoistic this term has no distinctive meaning. The same thing has often been said as to "matter" when the Materialist has affirmed that there is no "spirit,"—no opposite of matter. Matter then becomes synonymous simply with existence. The Materialist replies that he is content with the conclusion that there is no alleged existence unrelated to other and known existence; none exempt from manifestation according to a regular order or subject to the inherent law of its being, to speak according to appearances. There is a regular order of succession of phenomena. The Spiritual theory asserts a break in what is popularly called "the reign of natural law," Materialism denies such assertion and exists as a distinctive *ism* to deny and disprove it. This statement will indicate in part what is the proper reply when it is charged that Egoism is almost meaningless if it embrace all acts. It was believed that men acted disinterestedly. Closer examination finds the motive and the form of their interest. Thus a parallel to the progress made from the time when men believed in miracles to the time when they have learned enough of natural law to expel the former belief.

By referring to the definition already given of Egoism it will be seen that it covers a theory as well as facts. If every act of every animal were perfectly Egoistic, nevertheless the demands of intelligence would not be satisfied without understanding the phenomena, which are explained according to natural law as reactions of individual will to motives presented in circumstances. To act Egoistically is universal, but to be in part ignorant of the fact seems to be also nearly universal. The theory of Egoism has its opposite in the theory of Altruism, evidently joined to Spiritualism by ignoring and denying the necessary sequence in phenomena. (I make no allusion to modern Spiritualism, which professes to be Materialistic.)

But beyond this it can be firmly said that until the Egoistic theory is understood and has had its full influence upon character, those irrational actions will continue which are the fruit of error, illusion, fascination, fixed ideas, rendering the individual practically not an Ego,—not in the possession of his faculties,—hence there will be, as there are, actions not properly Egoistic, but insane, though not generally so understood. Thus the Egoistic theory has a practical purpose. The half insane,—that is to say all worshipers, religious, political or personal,—are to come to consciousness of their individuality and become wholly sane.

As to submissive actions performed simply under fear or hope, their Egoistic character is quite clear.

XII

The word right has the same fundamental meaning as straight. When no obstacle stands or lies between an animal and the object of its desire, the shortest way, which is a straight line, is the way the animal takes to reach the object; but when approach by a right line is impracticable the nearest known path is chosen, all considerations such as safety being weighed according to intelligence. This is then the line of least resistance,—the one most approximating in convenience to a right line. The right hand is so named because usually the stronger and more serviceable. A man's right is his straight way to the satisfaction of his desires, and he takes no other way except under adverse circumstances or hallucination.

It will be objected by Moralists that such an exposition of right reduces it to nothing but might. In this inference they are correct, but their objection does not disturb Egoistic philosophy, which regards their alleged supernal, sacred Right as a superstition. I have a right to what I can take and openly keep, and another has a right to take it from me if he can.

Those, however, who believe that a superior authority has laid down a rule to which they must conform, will take up that rule or law as they understand it, and their idea of right will be that of conformity to the command of the authority. The Moralist is under an impression that instead of pursuing his own pleasure he has to fulfill a purpose which may be at variance with his pleasure. His conception of Right is not an Egoistic conception. He has surrendered himself, and with himself his own right, and has begun to serve an abstraction. He is in the way to commit great folly and wrong to himself. To the Moralist Right and Wrong are two fixed ideas, forever in opposition in all senses. To the intelligent Egoist they are two words generally perverted from their meaning and used as scarecrows. There is a frequent clash between the right of one and the right of another, and they fight it out. It is settled by the triumph of one and the defeat of the other. Max Stirner in his matchless book, *The Ego and Its Own*, says: *Ist es mir recht, so ist es recht* (If it suits me, it is right.) The Moralist would say: if it be right for me; thus implying that he is under some mysterious authority. The Egoist would not use the latter preposition except when recognizing some law or definite arrangement which prescribes certain rights. When I say: "if it be right for me—," I admit an authority. Now in fact I must often admit one—, that is a power,—but I admit it simply as a power, not at all as the Moralist admits it. I do not bow down to it in my thought or regard it as anything but an enemy to my freedom, and if it cease to assert its power and to compel me by penalty or the prospect of penalty, I assert my full power to do my own pleasure and nothing but my own pleasure. The Moralist consents to serve as his own jailer; not so the Egoist. Assert your right, your power, your pleasure. I claim none of that, I assert my own. I appeal to no Moral law of the world. I recognize none. We shall find our interests coincide or we shall give each other battle or we shall steer clear of each other, according to circumstances.

In words you can assert my right, but when you attempt to do so in deeds you succeed only in asserting your own right. I alone can prove my right by deeds.

The Moralist pretends to be under an obligation to respect the rights of others and never do them any wrong; but he defines their rights and does not allow them all their rights. He abdicates his own and cripples theirs and then flatters himself that the mutilation and effacement constitute superior Right. He protests against Egoism because it wrongs his system. At times he imagines that the Egoist must talk in the language of Moralism and must mean that in acting with Egoistic right the Egoist would pretend not to do wrong to another; wherein the

Moralist becomes absurd, for the Egoist does not pretend that he can always exercise his right without wrong to another. It is a matter of expediency with the Egoist what wrong to another he shall do.

"Right wrongs no man," exclaims the landlord, and drives the tenant out of a house. The inclement weather beats upon the unsheltered, and their nerves are wrung. The landlord exercises his right, but lies moralistically.

The word *wrong* is a variation upon the past participle of the verb to *wring*, to twist. Victor and vanquished are two, and the Moralist simply looks away from the facts of life when he preaches a universal natural Right and ignores individuals with their various wants and powers and the probability that what is good to one may entail some ill upon another.

But the species? The Moralist, driven from the former position of a divinity ordering all things in harmony in the world, or at least the conceit that his own species is favored at the expense of all below it, and this not by its intelligence but by a divine decree arbitrarily making the spoilation of the world and rule over inferior animals Right, takes refuge in a belief that the welfare of the species may give Moral law to the individual. Hence the dogma that the individual exists for the species. Were it so, the individual might insist upon existing at any cost, assuming that he is what he knows best of the species, and that his stubborn will might probably be a provision for the species. That is Right, says the Moralist, which best serves the species. And what best serves the species? The Moralist will generally reply: "that which is Right," thus completing a little circle in dogmatism. Nature, however, seems to say that species survive by the survival of their individuals. The Egoist will find in himself certain loves and aversions, and he may think that the species is taking care of itself just in proportion as he is following those paths which give him satisfaction.

The Moralist, becoming more philosophical, suggests that the war of interests will cease as men understand their similar needs and the possibility of mutual benefit, hence wrongs in the species may become fewer or cease. With all our heart, say the Egoists, only you are not to begin by sacrificing us. If the later Moralism be merely a prophetic dream of a harmony of interests through wisdom, we are not without hope that at last the dreamers will recognize individuality as the condition precedent to the fulfillment of their hopes. The fellow feeling in the species is a certain fact. Let us take it for what we find it to be and not attempt to place it in antagonism to our individualities. As these are developed the necessity will appear for each one to recognize somewhat the individuals of his species, and thus the "claims of the species" will be recognized.

XIII

Self-interest masks itself and says suavely "we seek the good of the species," instead of saying bluntly, "we gladly pick up all that other individuals let slip from their grasp." Are not we the species as contradistinguished from any individual? When we go so far as to urge sacrifices for the good of the species what are we but beggars and hypocrites?

Persuasion is mingled freely with flattery administered to the vanity of the individual, and it is not to be ignored that the Moral philosopher flatters himself as he proceeds to render what he vainly imagines to be a service to his species. Assuming the point of view that he is spokesman for the species, the dictum that that is good conduct which promotes the interests of the species, is a subtle mendicancy or a veiled terror in the supposed interest of the crowd. But assuming an individual point of view the question is differently shaped. It then becomes: what use can I make of the species, of the crowd?

A summary of ethical teachings of Herbert Spencer says that postulating the desirability of the preservation and prosperity of the given species, there emerges the general conclusion that "in order of obligation the preservation of the species takes precedence of the preservation of the individual." The species he admits, "has no existence save as an aggregate of individuals," and hence "the welfare of the species is an end to be subserved only as subserving the welfare of individuals," but, continues the summary, "since disappearance of the species involves absolute failure in achieving the end, whereas disappearance of individuals makes fulfillment simply somewhat more difficult, 'the preservation of the individual must be subordinated to the preservation of the species where the two conflict.'"

There are several features of sophistry in this. Let us however, note first the admission that "the species" is simply a convenient term. Now, where confusion is possible the safe way is to lay aside the term. When this is done it will be found that in restating the foregoing propositions it becomes necessary to speak, instead, either of all the individuals concerned except one or of all the individuals concerned, without exception. But he has seemingly used the term species in both senses or else, with his "order of obligation," he has affirmed an obligation to subordinate the preservation of one individual to that of another. As this is intelligible for the purpose of the crowd dealing with individuals but not for the individual acting" for himself with himself as the victim, the immediate inference at this point is that Spencer is expounding the Egoistic logic of the crowd.

If the welfare of others is subserved only as subserving my welfare, it can never be true that I must subordinate my preservation to that of others, for this is to divert the general rule, which applies while I am one of the crowd, to the exceptional case wherein I am set apart from the crowd. All conditions of benefit imply at least preservation. When I am counted out for non-preservation, for the good of others, it must be the others, not I, who do the counting out. In the first premise Spencer speaks for the individual treating the crowd from his proper motive; but in the conclusion he speaks for the crowd or some of its preserved part contemplating the sacrifice of an individual, yet these shifting points of view are included in a syllogism. The welfare of the crowd a mediate end: that is reasonable to the individual. The preservation of the individual a mediate end to the crowd: that is reasonable from the crowd's point of view; but analysis of the diverse points of view is needed, not an attempt to link the two in a syllogism the conclusion of which is merely the crowd's conclusion.

Now examine the second premise of the syllogism: "the disappearance of the species involves absolute failure in achieving the end." Why, in fact? Because the disappearance of all others of the species but myself involves it? Not at all; but because the term species includes myself. But as far as my existence is concerned it would be the same if I alone disappeared. Do you say: the preservation of the alphabet is of no use to A except as A combines with other letters; but the disappearance of the alphabet would involve the disappearance of A; hence the preservation of one letter (A) is less important than the preservation of all the other letters? The letter A answers: "Bosh!"

Speaking for the individual, how does the doctrine of subordination of the preservation of the individual accord with evolutionary theory regarding; the origin of species? Do species originate by individuals taking care of themselves under whatever circumstances, if possible, or by the contrary rule of their benevolence toward the pre-existing species? The reader can pursue this inquiry for himself; but I should like to suggest that what has been considered regarding the individual and the species can be paraphrased with reference to the species and the genus under which it is classified, thus:

The welfare of the genus is to be subserved only as subserving the welfare of the species, but since the disappearance of the genus involves absolute failure, whereas disappearance of particular species makes fulfillment simply somewhat more difficult, therefore the preservation of the species must be subordinated to the preservation of the genus where the two conflict. The fallacy of this sort of reasoning may appear without comment, inasmuch as the individual will easily maintain the point of view of the interested species, and will not practically allow himself to slide over to the position of the presuming genus. A supplementary remark may be indulged. The genus never licenses or encourages the origination of new species; but then the verbal sophistry of the genus would not prove to be a preventive.

I pass by the small occasion of confusion in the use of the word "end," the second time, in the foregoing statement. Total failure may be assumed to refer to failure of the ultimate aim.

XIV

Duty is that which is due. I ought is I owe or I owed. Some duties I assume for duties assumed by others toward me. This is reciprocity. Some alleged duties the Moralist tells me that I ought to acknowledge and perform from a sense of Duty. If I then say that it is a superstition he perhaps severs himself for the moment from the superstitious crowd and claims that it is only a generalization, meaning fitness, saving tiresome repetition of analysis; it is my interest after all. He is somewhat disingenuous here, for if it be only my interest embodied in a thought-saving generalization, it will bear analysis and always come out as my interest. But he has the "social organism" in mind, to the preservation of which my individual welfare is to be subordinated, according to his idea. The "social organism" idea has captured him and he is using decoy argument to obtain from me a sacrifice of myself to his idol, his spiritual monster.

A man is hired to do certain work, and that is then called his duty; or exchange of services grows into a mutual understanding; the debt is first on one side and then on the other, and what at any time is expected, to balance the account or turn the scale as usual and create another claim so as to continue the mutually advantageous arrangement or understanding, is also called one's duty. Where service is compulsory it is likewise called duty.

Moralism, when it has gained enlightenment enough to reject slavery to a person, under the subjection of mind overawed by physical force, denies that the slave's duty is Duty. But if the slave has yielded his mind to his master the phenomenon is clearly that of Duty. When the Egoist is conscripted he does not argue that his assigned duty is not Duty. It is servitude contrary to his interest, and this consideration is enough. The fact that some slaves are governed by a sense of Duty furnishes the plainest evidence that Duty is mental slavery.

But the Moralist will claim for Duty that it is not always mental slavery. It is true that he can confuse the issue by using the word Duty to describe all those habitual actions in the doing of which no immediate benefit to self is thought of; but let us keep to the plain sense. Duty is what is due. The domination of a fixed idea begins when one admits something due and yet not due to any person or something due without benefit coming to one in return; and of course when a return benefit is calculated upon the idea is interest.

When interest is sublimated so as to lose sight of self it assumes the form of love in the absence of oppression. Evidently the presence of fear in the causative circumstances corrupts the sublimating process and results in the oppressive sense of Duty. It is possible for the Moralist, finding a series of admirable actions which are well-nigh perfect love or gratitude, to call these Duty, on an examination which will show that were the doer to study his conduct he could find in it the elements which would serve to construct a wise scheme of reciprocal duties. If the Moralist talks of Duty when the fact is spontaneity,—whether gratitude, love, overflowing pride or generosity advancing to aid all that is seen to make for our good, he talks at random. His system of thought has predicated that men need to be controlled by a sense of Duty. Let him stick to that or leave it. We deny it. The doctrine of hell-fire was long upheld under the same idea that it was needed to control men. Moralistic Duty is the hardened dregs of fear. Generosity is the overflowing fullness of a successful, satisfied and hopeful individuality.

"I ought" is no stumbling-block to the intelligent Egoist. Two persons are playing at draughts and a bystander says of one: "He ought to have captured the man to the left, not the one to the right." There is no sense of moral obligation conveyed in the remark. It is assumed that each player is trying to win, and the words "he ought" introduce a suggestion of what was wanting to produce the result. A pirate endeavoring to capture a merchantman and taking the wrong course would say: "I ought to have sailed on the other tack." To whom was the obligation? To himself. So men speak of their duty to themselves, meaning the attending to supplying what is lacking to their welfare.

These words *duty* and *ought* are not words to be rejected. They are in constant correct use in everyday life, and it is not the use of the Moralist, but it can be observed that every humbug politician harps on the "sacred duty" of the citizens to do this or that,— something that he and his party are interested in and that he cannot readily prove to be to the interest of the citizens addressed, or he would do so instead of trying to get them with him on an appeal to "sacred duty."

XV

The supposed inward monitor which warns the Moralist against breaking the sacred law of Right, as it admonishes the believer against offending God, is that which "doth make cowards of us all," in the language of the dramatist. That is conscience. One thinks he knows his Duty and with this thought come vague fear and self-reproach for not having obeyed the Moral law; not simple fear in the Moralist, rather a confused feeling, but a feeling as clearly distinguishable from the simple fear of consequences as Moralism is distinguishable from a calculation of interest. The dread is as undefined as the Authority or the reach of consequences, or both, are indefinite and dimly apprehended.

The fact that the dictates of conscience are the result of so-called "education" (really indoctrination) is established by the strongest proof on every hand. Every religion has its commandments and however absurd they may appear to others than the believers, conscience enforces their observance. Moralism continues in a general way the religious terror, making humanity or it may be more broadly animal life the sacred object.

Egoism, on the contrary, regards conscience as superstition. It is true that by simple analysis of the word, which yields *con*, with, and *science*, knowledge, we can have the definition: the sensation, sentiment or reflection regarding ourselves which accompanies knowledge of our voluntary action. But as an Egoist has simply either satisfaction or regret and does not judge himself by reference to any standard of Duty, he cannot have a guilty conscience.

It is most to the purpose, therefore, of Egoistic philosophy to look into the means of destroying the superstitious habit, for it is a notorious fact that self-condemnation continues somewhat after reason has assured the subject of the error of the doctrine which claimed his allegiance.

A silly conscience is to be extinguished, like other inconvenient habits, by resolute action. I have known a compositor who seemingly could not place a letter in line without first making an unnecessary motion with it against the side of his composing stick; a statesman who could not or dared not go to bed without first placing his boots as he wore them; a youth whose reason rejected the orthodox Christian doctrines in which he had been reared but who had qualms, which surprised him, about studying on Sunday; an infidel who had killed a man but had nothing to fear from the law, who nevertheless had the horrors in his dreams, and several persons with freelove ideas but inconsistent in practice in a way that showed the rule of their old conscience. Some of these things will strike everyone as being ridiculous. Of the instances cited only one did not admit of correction by Emerson's rule of doing the thing you fear to. I firmly believe that if the man who had a life on his conscience had taken the rational method of doing all else which he knew to be sensible, his mind would have been much strengthened to overcome his trouble of blood-guiltiness. The Sunday school young man realized that his conscience was awry, or the habit of a superstitious belief, and in a moderate time he overcame it. Others have had similar experiences as to books and conversation of a "blasphemous" character and breaches of the so-called law of morality in the sexual relation. Reasoning is well in its place, but action is necessary to make a free man or woman when one has been trained to have a conscience in any particular. I mean only action which combines pleasure with safety. It is no part of philosophic Egoism to pay more for advancement than it is worth.

XVI

The origin of the guilty conscience may be in mishaps, such as defeat, capture and slavery. When men from exercising mastery and even cruelty, are subjected to the rule of the stronger and more warlike, their energies are turned inward in bitterness against themselves. Upon this gnawing of ill humor comes the suggestion from religious belief, that these uncomfortable feelings are sent by the tribal god as a warning. This is readily believed by people who already believe that defeat and misfortune are punishments for some lapse of duty to their deity. The checking of an active career and humbling of the vanquished produce a bilious temper and morbid spirit, ready for ascetic rites on misdirection, because ever ready to attribute misfortunes to something other than their simple natural causes.

The guilty conscience precedes the good conscience. The latter is nothing but the consciousness of the guilty conscience removed—by expiation, atonement or however beliefs run.

Before the guilty conscience there was the spontaneity of the free savage. After the guilty and the good conscience there is the serenity of the self-conscious, sovereign, intelligent Ego. For convenience I will hereafter speak of him simply as the Egoist. While all men are Egoists in so far as they are not visionaries or madmen, nearly all men are in fact partly blinded, ashamed of themselves, not fully possessed of themselves. They do things for conscience sake—Egoistic method in madness;—they reject religious doctrine, but have a "sense of sin;" they have a horror of certain acts because condemned by a "moral standard," and so forth. They do not even understand that they cannot be "sinners" except by admitting a religious standard of "righteousness;" that they cannot be "immoral," wicked, without thinking as saints and Moralists think of "guilt," "disobedience" in natural acts. They cannot even call themselves Egoists to their satisfaction because the religious world has branded every natural impulse as vile and "unsanctified;" consequently Egoism—self-direction—as the sum of all villainy, and they are hampered by accepting their language from the religious world.

The real Egoist is not even he who has merely seen through the cheat of Moralism, but he who has outgrown its habitual sway, broken its scepter, desecrated every shrine of superstition in his heart or else been more happily born and reared than one in ten thousand of those who live today or ever lived.

XVII

The Egoist hears voices saying: "Forgive us our sins." His thought takes a humorous turn and he asks: Why do not the idiots think of forgiving themselves each one his own sins? Why cannot they be like the father? If "I and my father are one," I can do the acts of the father and forgive my own sin. He who dare not say: "I do most cheerfully forgive myself all sins and misdeeds I have ever committed or shall ever care to commit," is certainly not an Egoist.

Moralists propound the question: "Does the end justify the means?" He who argues on either side of it, shows not the quality of Egoism. It is a question for Moralists, to be answered by reference to their standards of duty. The Egoist will ask whether the game is worth the powder and in this sense he could use the very words quoted in the question; meaning, however, only a particular application of means to a particular end—a question of expenditure or risk and probability of gain. Every case being decided on the principle of economy or of strategy, the general moral question disappears. The Moralist is left to answer his own question as to whether or not he will venture to break a "moral law" in order to accomplish what he considers a moral good.

Another way of putting our criticism is that the question can be parodied: "Does the evidence warrant the verdict?" But then, you say we must know what verdict and what evidence are referred to. Quite so; and the question: "Does the end justify the means?" is equally void of meaning unless we learn what end is sought and what means are proposed.

But suppose we become more specific and ask: "Is the killing of a heretic justified by the probability of saving one thousand souls from perdition?" To this I say it concerns the Moralist, not the Egoist. In order to kill, no justification before the tribunal of conscience is necessary to, say, the Egoistic statesman; for that is a piece of superstition. In this respect "all things are lawful" for him, "but all things are not expedient." The heretic has to thank the thousand other heretics for his immunity from being killed for heresy. A common interest unites them in some measures for self-protection. Their danger is but the greater because fanatics exist who in addition to the brutal instincts of mankind are possessed with the idea of a moral pardoning power encouraging men to do violence as a service, not to themselves but to a creed of church or society. The Egoist wastes no breath to persuade the fanatic that the end would not justify the means. He knows that the wish was father to the thought. The doctrine of exceptional justification was the inevitable excuse, like the wolf's brief remarks to the lamb at the stream. That wolf was not a natural wolf, but a moralizing wolf; still, altogether a wolf in fact. The moralizing man is less frank and more cunning than the wolf. He would paralyze his enemies by teaching that not all courses are "justifiable;" then when they spare him and he gets them in his power he does not spare them. The end never justifies the means when a Moralist is being hurt: always when a Moralist is getting the best of the fight by unusual artifice and usurpation.

XVIII

The idea of injustice precedes that of justice. Dr. Maurice de Fleury in his book, *L'Ame du Criminel*, says: Assuming the legend of Cain and Abel to be true, the brothers had a quarrel and when Cain struck Abel, the latter struck back. The fight continued for some time. Just when Abel was directing a blow, his arm was struck and fell helpless by his side. The impulse to deliver the blow returned to the brain as consciousness of purpose frustrated and this was the first sense of that want of correspondence which is called injustice.

If at such a juncture a tree or rock should happen to fall upon the victor or a lion make him his prey, and the vanquished escape, the latter would thank a supposed providential interference, build an altar and found a worship.

Out of a great number of cases of hurts—injustice—the sufferers build such theory of justice as corresponds with their idea of the satisfaction of their demands.

"Just right" is what fits a place or case. Adjustment and even justification are words used in a mechanical sense. Justice, however, cannot be predicated till we come to relations between persons. It is evident that in the notion or sentiment of justice there are present two elements: first, fitness in general, as in common with accuracy; secondly a recognition of something more, which may be the sentient nature of the object. We do not speak of injustice save where there is a possibility of suffering.

There are a great many applications of the term justice, but in all of them it has some relation to sentient beings and to fitness. The differences apparently spring from different standards of authority, rules of privilege, right, immunity, etc. Every uproar among men is a proof of injustice, in the same way as the creaking or screeching of a machine is an evidence of parts ill adjusted.

The loudest advocates of justice complacently overlook the

fact that nobody extends justice to the inferior animals.

The adjustment of relations between man and man will probably be best where each one is alive to his own interests and convenience. In the absence of this condition justice is the warcry in quixotic campaigns, the success of which in any instance serves to destroy some privilege and emancipate some ignorant, helpless folk to become tools of fanatics and victims of speculators. The free are those who free themselves. These and these only can or will do themselves justice and they are prevented from doing themselves and each other justice most of all by the prevailing belief in justice as a "ruling principle." The motto: "Let justice be done though the heavens fall," is a perfect example of fanaticism, equal to insisting on some one performance, though any amount of loss and suffering results. But the very men who harp on justice are the ones who delegate the trial and execution to functionaries chosen haphazard, and make a religious duty of submitting to injustice whenever these functionaries are ignorant, corrupt, prejudiced or mistaken in their judgment. The idea that any person might do himself justice, though no doubt existed that the act were justice, is horrifying to the good socialists, because the executioner was not appointed by society. Justice, then, is a prerogative of society, a favor rather than a right, in their view. They become involved in perplexities. The heavens may fall, but not the dignity of the state. They deny justice to save respect for its mechanism. An unjust law is enforced by the same authority which enforces a just law. It is enforced, all knowing that it is unjust, and because it is unjust, to the end that it may be repealed. Somebody is made a victim of injustice in order that by forcible wrong, thus done by authority, another branch of authority may be induced to alter a decree and issue another decree (which will be certain to accomplish another wrong to somebody).

Revenge is not justice, but simply the impulse to do hurt for hurt. It lacks measure, balance. It is at most a propensity which makes for the extermination or humbling: of aggressors.

The Egoist does not worship justice. He recognizes the impossibility of its existing as a donation. The ruler or the society which decrees justice is the shepherd who manages his flock, not for the sake of the flock, but for his interest in it. The Egoist aims at the accommodation of interests according to the capacity of the contracting parties. Egoist with Egoist must recognize, and on reflection will rejoice at the prospect of a rule of not trespassing where—he had better not. From this he can arrive at a position of comfort in having allies of great value to him, through their not being afflicted with any superstition. They multiply his power and he adds to theirs.

As to justice in the sense of meting out punishment to persons according to their alleged moral delinquencies, the idea gives place to that of protecting ourselves and serving our convenience. We may suppress a dangerous madman and a dangerous sane man as a measure of prevention, not having the old Moralistic horror of responsibility in the case of ourselves dealing with the madman, and not having the Moralistic furor against the sane offender. We need not therefore resort to casuistry* in case of slight doubt if we are determined that it is unsafe to risk permitting either to live. Thus Egoists will not let an offender off on technicalities or scruples if they deem it necessary to expel him or kill him, and thus, too, if one has killed another the inquiry will be as to whether or not the slayer merely anticipated an intelligent verdict by a jury.

Let us beware of the craze for justice. It is the mask of social tyranny. It demands a delegated authority and a prerogative in this authority. Thus it builds a citadel of injustice; so that the man who does himself justice is declared by the law to be guilty of a crime against it, the monopoly of administration of justice.

---

* *Casuistry* is the resolving of specific cases of conscience, duty, or conduct through interpretation of ethical principles or religious doctrine. [ed.]

XIX

What of equal liberty? Egoism is interior liberty, which of course makes for equal liberty of Egoists. But this is on the basis of their common ability, whereas democracy and aristocracy have a common principle in the affirmation of birthright: In democracy liberty is the sacred birthright of every man. In aristocracy liberty and privilege are the right of those born or admitted to aristocratic rank. The spirit of democracy is, to fashion each individual on its model, and endow him with political equality in contradistinction to class privileges, but as a member of the democracy into which his passport is his humanity, not his personal assertion and demonstration of his power and will to command equal liberty. Aristocracy commands its members to maintain their rank. Democracy commands its members to maintain an equal status for all. Egoism awaits the coming of the free, who will recognize each other, but not by virtue of any birthright.

Contrasts between men as lions and lambs, eagles and doves, are fanciful and overdrawn. Nature has not endowed them with such extreme and transmissible differences of organism. When they shake off old beliefs and indoctrination and realize their powers as individuals, equal liberty follows from the practically equal assertion of similar physical powers in self-conscious Egoism. When each of us has determined to be as free as he can, to yield only to effective force in restraint of the liberty he wills to exercise, there will be more liberty and substantially equal liberty for us if we be numerous, even while far from a majority.

The idea of liberty for man as Man, as something to be respected for its own sake, though the man be a slavish animal,—the sacredness of Man,—is a different notion altogether. While I am, indeed, an example of man in general, I base my claim to consideration at the hands of Egoists on the fact of my being this man who can be known to be neither tyrant whom they must combat nor slave incapable of requiting their aid. I will be a useful ally for certain purposes. I will not spend my strength in contending for equal guardianship, miscalled equal liberty, but I will seek allies like-minded. Not knowing whether I shall find one yonder in a born aristocrat or there in a toiling plebeian, I will put out the sign of equal liberty to exist among allies and of a readiness to take allies for equal liberty as a working rule, not as a religion.

Republicans think they abolished the community of plebeians when they abolished aristocratic rank. Far from it. They reduced the aristocrats to the plebeian level before the law and set up an aristocracy of office-holders and of wealth, which traffics in the making and administration of the laws. Equal liberty remains entirely unknown, because liberty is unknown as an objective reality. There can be no liberty of action till it is understood that each of us finds his law in his will and pleasure and that wherein our wills and pleasures agree we make our law, which we enforce on others who come into our domain, because we must or it is our convenience so to do. Thus only, liberty and law are synonymous. Be not unequally yoked together with non-Egoists. They cannot maintain your liberty. Your right and liberty, apart from what you can do for yourself, is that part of your will and pleasure which receives the support of allies lending you the aid of their power, as their right and liberty has the same extension by recognition and aid from you and others. The Egoist does not commit the mistake of battling for emancipation and endowment with power, misnamed equal liberty, of a herd of human cattle. More precious to me than ten thousand of these is one person capable of asserting all attainable liberty. Still, I came from the herd and by this and like signs I know that the herd contains my precious allies in the making. I send, among those who can hear, the word of awakening. Come to me and I will recognize in you equal liberty; I will give myself, if you will, a duty toward you, to be performed on pain of losing your esteem and support. I have already the pleasure of seeking and the hope of finding you. Life is worth less without you than it will be with you. Your precious force is my strength from the moment that you understand that I have no greater hope than in your fullest assertion of your liberty. We will not allow the world to wait for the overman. We are the overmen.

Aristocracy has not that fascination for me that it has for F. Nietzsche. Whatever pleasure a man may feel in wielding power in association with bold and strong companions, a reflecting man must despise an hereditary system which is subject to the following defects: that in order to transmit power to one of his sons he must consent to place his other sons in an inferior position; that he must aid in maintaining a special prerogative for the degenerate sons of his original colleagues; that he must give his daughters to such inferior scions to be their marital slaves; that to support the system he must aid in employing those vermin, the priests; that to keep down the plebeians he must slay many a brave and intelligent fellow of plebeian birth.

XX

One can feign a selfish motive to obtain opportunity to do an act of personal kindness; that is, one feigns one self-interested purpose in order to accomplish another self-interested purpose—to overcome the pride of independence in another person. A number of the most delightful stories have this point. The generosity which thus disguises itself differs fundamentally from abstract philanthropy or theoretical Altruism. The reader perceives in every such story how thoroughly the generous heart enjoys its success in aiding particular persons of merit who have attracted its good will. But one never feigns a selfish interest in order to do a disinterested act. On the other hand, how well mankind know that hypocrites profess disinterestedness while their aims are selfish.

In the generous act there is spontaneous, personal motive; no dread duty; no bending before a master power. Do you say the master power is there? Well, it comes through the doer's individual organism as a genial impulse, interesting him, and so is Egoistic. Do you complain that thus we make of Egoism what you call selfishness and what you call unselfishness? We show you that there is a common element of genuine personality, even of pleasurable action, in both. Opposite are the acts in which the person yields his will, subjugated by an ideal, the powers of which are awe, dread and lashing duty. I do not care to quarrel about a word with those whose idea is beckoning-duty. If it comes through my sense of what is worthy of me, due to fulfill my honor and dignity, that too is distilled in my consciousness or subconsciousness and is of my aliment and flowering and of the fruitage of my sentiment, intellect and will—is Egoistic.

XXI

Since the publication of these chapters began, I have seen in libertarian papers several flippant remarks and attempted refutations. We hear that Egoism is a very old thing, which is true; but that is one cause why the sour critics have missed understanding it, for they have gone to old books in which they found the idea of Egoism as viewed in the fight of the science, philosophy and politics of past ages; or they have gathered opinions from superficial writings. Many show absolutely no understanding of Egoism. It is an affair of objective classification of acts, they suppose. Thus if I have an apple and eat it, that is Egoism, they suppose. If I give the apple to my friend, that is Altruism, they suppose. How simple! Then I, being an Egoist and liking to see some of my friends eat my apples, must not indulge in this pleasure unless I can stand certain persons' charges of inconsistency. Let me give them a point: I select my friends. My apples are not for everybody to help himself. Let me give them another point. The man who eats his own apple, not because he likes it, but because he thinks it is Egoistic to eat it,—not to talk of duty,—is only a deluded Egoist, by which I mean that he has missed being an Egoist in the definite sense in which I am using the word in these closing chapters.

One correspondent demolishes Egoism thus: that Egoism is Hedonism or Eudemonism, the pursuit of pleasure; that it is absurd to say that the pleasure of professing Christianity outweighed the pain of being burned at the stake; that hence it is not true that the pursuit of pleasure is the greatest motive.

"The pursuit of pleasure," is an expression which has conveyed to many persons the idea that Egoism consists for all men in satiating certain appetites; but the truth is that philosophically "pleasure" stands for sovereignty—is used in contradistinction to servitude.

Egoists do not accept the state of mind of a Christian martyr as being normal. He believed that a crown of glory awaited those faithful to death; that exclusion from the presence of the Lord awaited the "apostate." Qualified by these beliefs undoubtingly held, how can we deny the martyr's (deluded) Egoism? The apostolic "fishers for men" baited their hooks with promises and threats addressed to self-interest and repeated: "Fear not them that kill the body," etc. Are only those who secure good bargains to be credited with the intention to secure them?

The critic makes a ludicrously false comparison when he sets the physical pain of burning against the mental pain of apostasy. At the moment when the Christian martyr made choice of constancy to his religion and a crown of glory, he had not felt the physical agony of having his flesh consumed by fire. As much as possible he fixed his thought on the promised heaven and thus lessened the anticipation of pain. Whatever pain there was in the expectation of burning it was not the pain of actual burning. We do not know what the final suffering was nor what the final thoughts were. We read of one on the cross, when too late, exclaiming: "My God, my God! Why hast thou forsaken me?" and we read that the servant shall not be above his lord. Moreover if the Christian martyr could be supposed to fully appreciate the pain of the death that awaited him, he must also be supposed to appreciate as fully the hell which awaited the apostate and endless death in the lake of fire. How then must such a terrified believer decide on the Egoistic principle as distorted by his faith? To us there is no more difficulty in his case than there is in the principle of gravitation illustrated by a ball rolling down an inclined plane when that is the nearest approach it can make to perpendicular descent.

But while we may suppose a martyr possibly logical in his course, given his absurd belief, we feel warranted in thinking that the majority of those who sought martyrdom were excited beyond the control of reason, as is the case with men acting under the dominion of passion in the commission of certain offences. Craziness is essentially an inability to weigh conditions and apprehend consequences.

Another thinks that Egoism kills sympathy and thus, he thinks, hinders the care of children.

The prevailing opinion that general betterment depends upon increased sympathy is one which I am more and more decided to pronounce a stupendous error. Sympathy diverts energy from one channel to turn it into another. An illustration showing the ruin caused by an irrational excess of grief may cause some to re-examine their opinion. B was married three years ago. Lately his wife died, leaving a child a year old. B was so much affected by the death of his wife that he went to the cemetery day after day and lay down on the ground crying. There he contracted an infectious disease and he also died, thus leaving the child an orphan.

Another is shocked at Egoism, as it has no reverence for anything sacred, not even for Feuerbach's jugglery that "love is divine" and "man is godlike" or can be by thinking himself so. Also that Egoism puts no premium on "courage" but rather on cowardice.

It is well to be shocked in default of any other way of getting intelligence awakened. Be sure that Egoism has nothing sacred, and therefore accepts no imposture or hallucination and remember that it requires courage to be a coward and appear a coward. Where "courage" is folly, it is Egoistic to be a "coward." Certainly it is only Egoism that can ridicule sacred things of man as well as of God: I mean ridicule in action as well as in word. Pecksniff,* even if an Atheist in woman's clothes, should be snubbed, and the Egoist will snub him, without regard to his or her sex.

* In the original this is written as "Pecknilf", though my best guess is this may refer to "Pecksniff", a Dickens character known for being a hypocrite who pretends to be pious and love his fellow man, but is a liar and who treats others cruelly. [ed.]

XXII

What is good? What is evil? These words express only appreciations. A good fighter is a "good man," or a "bad man!" both words expressing the same idea of ability, but from different points of view. To the beggar a generous giver is a good man. To the master a servant is good when he cheerfully slaves for the master. A good subject is one obedient to his prince. A good citizen is one who gives no trouble to the state, but contributes to its revenues and stability. Evil is only what we do not find to our good, but what we have to combat. A horse is not good because strong and swift if he be "vicious;" that is, if we find him hard to tame. A breed of dogs is good if readily susceptible of training to hunt all day or watch all night for the benefit of the owner. A wife is "good" if she will not be good to any man but her husband.

Why do the lion and the eagle enjoy such a reputation? The eagle attacks nobody except babes. The lion is a large animal, deliberate in his movements and reputed to give a man a chance to get away. There are "worse" animals.

In all varieties of Moralism obedience is the cardinal virtue, which is wholly on the principle of procuring "good" subjects for those who have the effrontery to set up as rulers over fools and simpletons. "Be good and you will be happy." "Virtue is its own reward." These proverbs are an appeal to self-interest beguiled to accept some current teaching as to what is "good" conduct, "virtue." What if one be happy and healthy and the same believers in these maxims tell him that his happiness is not good? They show that their idea of goodness is obedience to certain commands or rules. But the Egoist will prove most things and hold fast to that which he finds to be good for him. That which he finds to be "its own reward" he holds to be—virtue enough. The positions are opposites. The Moralist says: "This course is virtue;

believe it and follow instructions, and you will find happiness in the thought of doing right." The Egoist perceives that such instruction is a trap for credulity. The experience of mankind is all very well, but most of the time your Moralist deprecates experiment. It is remarkable that in "the most important relation in life" two persons must make a legal contract for permanent union before they have any knowledge of each other in the relation; then bear it if they dislike it, and this is regarded as virtue. I do not say that all Moralists teach such doctrine, but all Moralists have some doctrine which they enforce by sentiment demanding individual sacrifice, absolutely and not merely as individually expedient.

XXIII

Truth, the agreement between thinking and thing,—between thought and *that*,—is as desirable as seeing and hearing without illusion or confusion. Truth, the agreement between thinking and expression, is made a duty by Moralists, yet generally with reservations. May a man lie to assassins to save his life, or to robbers to save treasure committed to his care, or to a sick person to conceal news which would be a serious shock? The gravity with which such questions are argued points to something further,—that Truth, like Right and Justice, is erected into a deity and men go crazy or pretend to go crazy over the worship thereof. This is the hypocrite's opportunity. So people bind themselves with an oath and lend a spurious importance to words spoken by men who care only for immunity, but who are shrewd enough not to profess what they think and how independent they feel.

How curious that men generally feel it "right" to cut and hack natural forms, but not to take any liberty with "truth" even in the verbal representation of such forms!

But on the other hand they say: "All's fair in love and war." Now everything that is not love can be viewed as war (and the "love" here spoken of is war too). This maxim is more often used to excuse lying than for any other purpose. Lying is a very common practice and I perceive no reason to expect it's abatement unless individuals in large numbers (1) cease to pretend to exact from others action which is inconvenient, when they cannot or do not really exact it; (2) make it to the interest of others to tell them the truth or leave others alone as to telling anything about matters on which they now tell lies. So there might be less "war."

To the Egoist truth is an economy, where practicable. The chief condition is mutual intelligence.

Honesty,—truth in action,—is commonly said to be "the best policy," and perhaps as commonly disbelieved to be unconditionally so. Where honesty is reciprocal, it brings that mutual advantage which attaches to truthfulness, but honest conduct in an individual in dealing with dishonest persons, is too simple. Honesty is a pleasure, often a luxury.

XXIV

Moralism reaches its acme in the craze for a supposed perfection the opposite way from individuality. Even when philosophy has pronounced that its aim is to lead man to find himself, the spirit of perversion is such that it takes Man, the general idea of the species, as an ideal for the individual and teaches individuals to torture their personal mind in order to conform to the idea formed about the species. Thus it is said our "mission" is to be true men, more perfect men, more perfect women. This notion prompts to imitation of what has been exemplified in others, not to development of that which is most genuinely myself or yourself. If I am to be a conforming man, striving to be something set before me, I cannot be I. As Stirner remarks, "every man who is not deformed is a true or perfect man, but each one is more than this. He is this unique man." What he is that another is not, we cannot say in advance of knowing him. Egoism is this: that this man acts out himself. Every woman may be assumed to be a true or perfect woman, and she is cheated if taught to assume otherwise. That is not the aim; that is the starting point with us Egoists. Be easy about perfection of Man. The individual needs first to be free from any yoke or assigned task, in order to normally possess, enjoy, develop and exhibit himself or herself. I shall develop the species, if I have nothing more distinctive to develop. A woman will be merely a "true and perfect woman" if she has nothing of her own, only of the species. The very moment, however, that she knows herself to be already a "true and perfect woman," as the zero or horizon of individuality, that moment is the individual energy set free to work out whatever it takes pleasure in,—or as free as conscious reflection can make us while old habits and affections persist in some degree. To come to ourselves, to find ourselves, is to know that what we have of the species is ours, so far as it suits us to keep it and that we have neither obligation nor mission but what each one may give himself.

XXV

A woman is—possibly an Egoist. Apart from this possibility she is—simply a female. If an Egoist, she will determine her actions with precisely that interior freedom possessed by the male Egoist.

Marriage, whether as polygamy or monogamy, is an agreement among men in a given state to respect each other's property in one or more women, according to the law of the tribe or state. It depends upon deluded Egoism. The supposed happiness of exclusive possession as a right to be enforced is resolvable into several factors such as (1) The certain immediate desire for possession; (2) The notion that the person possessed is passive and a constant quantity; (3) The seeming accumulation of happiness by monopolizing that which others would use if permitted, the defeating of their desire being supposed to be the securing of one's own. Some men, however, marry because they see that the desired woman will be married by another and hence lost to them unless they take her on the customary contract.

Men flatter themselves that they can perpetuate themselves and not merely the race; a simple error, for if we allow half the effect to each parent, the result is that A's offspring is half A; his grandchild is one-fourth A; his great-grandchild is one-eighth A; the next generation one-sixteenth A, and thus his descendants will have nothing more in common with him than any of the individuals of his race.

Some learned men argue that while men are naturally polygamous, women are naturally monogamous; but their discourse soon turns into censure of any woman who does not come up to the mark, as being a perverted creature. Are they blind to the vast amount of fear, reserve and duplicity in women? Can the subjugation of woman through all past time have failed to make her seem and act as though her nature were different from man's? Is not the watch kept upon her a proof that the preachers have no deep faith in her nature being different from their own? But what would be the fate of an author who should terrify society by assimilating the nature of the two sexes, while affirming man's polygamous instinct? He would be accused of a tendency to corrupt virtuous womanhood.

All agree that jealousy is a cruel and tormenting passion. Is it not, then, self-evidently a sign of perverted Egoism? The temper which is not jealous, which can love and let love, and enjoy the love that is spontaneously given because attracted, is undoubtedly happier than the jealous disposition. Such a temper will be willing to let the nature of woman display itself in freedom, and not until more of such a temper is shown is it to be expected that men will be privileged to know from women what women really are.

The wife enjoys a status. To forfeit it is to forfeit reputation. The husband is judged differently. It looks as if the modern woman, for the present, were mostly contenting herself with keeping her reputation and using the status in which man has placed her, for what there is in it. Liberty is not hers, but some power she can wield. Such power cannot fail to be a curtailing of the husband's resources, liberty or convenience, honesty, growth; and if he is fool enough to presume too far on his prerogative, he is sure in many instances to be deceived, for woman's wit has been forced in the direction of deception as much as to submission. The latter implies the former.

With the discovery by men that the perpetuation of their individuality is an illusion, that the expectation of happiness by the exercise of authority over woman is a gross mistake, that the person possessed is not a constant quantity but a variable one, a good to be elicited by wise treatment and not by rule of thumb. Egoism comes into the relation of the sexes, without delusion. The woman will have her way in the matter of procreation and will have the control of her children till they are wise enough to assert the control of themselves.* What have we onlookers to do with the relations of mother and infant? Nothing.

Those who are in the married state sometimes pretend that if they were single they would remain single. They are not to be believed because they say so. Marriage to very many is a sacred thing in some aspect or the demon of deluded selfishness is stronger than they confess. What if we say to them: Please for a moment regard your marriage as the marriage of a pair of doves or canaries. When so regarded what is there to talk about in the question whether you are married or not, apart from bare legal powers?†

Related to this is the idea that crimes of jealousy, even outside of marital relations, can be traced to the idea of marital rights. The man and woman who have cohabited have talked

* Will the Union of Egoists legislate on the "debt" of grown children to their mother? Our Union will be based simply on our common interests. The interest must be clear to each Unit in order to command support for any rule. Only a minority can have a pecuniary interest in the above suggested claim. We may first eliminate all the men, as the children belong only to the mothers. We can also leave out all the women who have no children that are under our jurisdiction or likely to come under it, and those mothers who are content with the unrestricted control of their infant children to train and impress them as they will; content to blame themselves if a child proves ungrateful after ten or fifteen years of such opportunity to form its disposition. To my thinking the policy of awarding compensation in after years, would imply the policy of interfering with the mother's absolute control over the child during infancy, for in this control lies the making or spoiling of the child's character. I prefer to trust her entirely and leave her to face the results of her training of her child.

† You say certain birds are monogamous and that this argues that man may be so. Accept the assurance that Egoists will be content to see the question resolved by the free play of instinct in the species, as you suggest. But the action of mankind, by legislation and social censure on the matter, looks very like a confession that they regard themselves as naturally constituted with an inclination to variety in love and needing a deal of dragooning to make them good monogamists or passable counterfeits thereof.

or thought of marriage and come to regard their connection as a marriage without the ceremony. Marriage and the possibility of marriage are in this way responsible for those crimes which simulate marital vengeance.

Some people contrast love with selfishness. They surely cannot mean sexual love. *Te quiero* is translated either "I love thee" or "I want thee." By common understanding love that is not selfish enough to break some law in order to satisfy a personal want, is not strong enough to hold a spirited mate.

Others find in sex an argument against Egoism. They say you cannot be an independent individual, because you are incomplete without one of the opposite sex. We may reply that a man is very much sooner done for if deprived of food or water than if unable to meet with an agreeable woman; consequently if there were anything in the above argument it would lead to the conclusion that the having any physical requirements militates against Egoism. But, on the contrary, we find they all afford scope for Egoism. We are likely to find in our surroundings the objects essential to our existence, and this comes out with regard to companionship just as with regard to materials for food, clothing and shelter. Egoism lies entirely in our attitude toward objects, not in our being constituted to have no need of them. We cannot fly, and we are subject to hunger and other appetites. Our needs serve to awaken our powers to activity and give various occasions for converting threatened suffering into enjoyment, if we meet everything in a thoroughly intrepid, Egoistic spirit. Even our need of social conversation is no derogation from Egoism. The man who uses and appropriates to himself the benefit of intercourse with others—of his choosing—is an intelligent Egoist, whereas the shrinking, solitary man is weaker: he attaches too much importance to something and he permits it to drive him from the field of activity and enjoyment.

Theoretically and practically the position of a married

woman is in all essential respects the opposite of that which an Egoist would choose. Still, there is no position in which one may accidentally find oneself (short of actual imprisonment) that can make any difference to the individual comparable in effect to the difference between Egoism (mental liberty) and non-Egoism (mental slavery).

If a woman had sold herself into chattel slavery which the law forbids, she would feel no hesitation in repudiating the bargain. What is the difference in marriage? The difference lies in the social sanction. The victims await emancipation by social opinion. This is not Egoism, but its opposite.

XXVI

Reared in Evangelical Christianity I passed, between the ages of 15 and 18, through the stages of Biblical criticism and disbelief in Providence, on the ground of the supremacy of natural law, to Atheism.

As my religion had been an undoubting faith in and obedience to an ideal Ego—God—when I unbound myself from the web of theology, I fell heir to the sovereign attributes,—the liberty and the benevolence,—of the God who then became a myth. I did not cheat myself a day with Moral commandments without a Moral Lawgiver. Yet I felt and foresaw that what was gained by the intellect would not be easily translated into feeling and action for many years to come, such was the Moral susceptibility and force of habits, from early indoctrination. I said to myself as a youth: "I feel that not until I am 40 years of age shall I be able to act in all things as my judgment decides for my own interest." It was even so.

Thus in the first half of the sixties I was an Atheist and self-conscious Egoist. I associated with Atheists and took part in their propaganda before I was 20 and for years after. But I found a false note among the Atheists, that theirs was the religion of Humanity with a Morality not less impressive upon the conscience than that connected with theology, purer because freed from superstition. They challenged comparison as to the Morality of their leaders and members with Christians,—the Christian standard being usually implied as to what constituted Morality. There were among them men impressed with the philosophy of Epicurus, of Hobbes, of D'Holbach and Spinoza,—self-love as the foundation and sum of morals, but the drift of their discourses was that good morals would grow out of self-love,—and still the morals were Christian morals. When an Atheist ceased to take an interest in the iconoclastic propaganda, he usually settled down into a selfish individual, a nonentity of ordinary morals. His Egoism was after the current ideas of rudimentary Egoism which orthodox Moralists propagate and his former associates simply regretted that he was no longer militant or contributory to the Atheistic church.

From the first of my mental independence, or Atheism, I repudiated conscience and a Moral standard; and I was equally dissatisfied with the attempted limitation of self-love, to grubbing for advantages over other people; certain that it was purely my pleasure or prudence which impelled me to any act, I declared in print, prior to 1870, that when an Atheist acts honestly toward another person it is because it is his pleasure to do so. This aroused a critic who affirmed the "sense of justice" governing Atheists. A pretty term, but when we have arrived at a "sense of justice" why do we inconvenience ourselves for it? I affirm a pleasure, a sentiment of good will and of art. There is no "must" about it with the Egoist. But with my Atheistic critic there was a spice of dictation, as who should say "you must *yield* to a sense of Duty to Humanity." Hard by lurks bigotry.

Feuerbach's inversion of theology, turning "God is love," into "love is divine," did not fascinate me. I saw in it a play on words. In my infancy God was a stern fact and when he became a myth, why, love was—love, not divine; goodness was what we find to make for our good; that is to say there was nothing divine; no such thing as goodness or badness except as relative to our welfare and no better reason why I should not be a cruel man than that I took no pleasure in cruelty, found no sense in it.

I have always rather pitied those who run passionately after the so-called good things which Christians and Moralists generally suppose must be the sole aim of Egoists. What fools are the fretful lusters after power, men covetous of others' goods, toilsome accumulators of what they cannot enjoy! Deluded Egoists!*

* A dwarfed, stunted conception of Egoism finds expression in the remark: "I do not believe in self-interest. I would not take another man's

During the period I have mentioned and until the spring of 1872 I had no knowledge of Max Stirner's work, *The Ego and Its Own*. But believe me that I devoured it so soon as I got hold of it. There for the first time I saw most plainly stated, my own thought, borne out by illustrations that will test the nerve of every professed Egoist. Who but Stirner has dared to suggest that the tie of blood is a superstition? Were it not that we have assurance of the speedy appearance of an English translation of his great work, I would here give something of a summary of its contents; but now, under the pleasing expectation, I may confine myself to a mention of one feature of that wonderful book. The author shows us the world divided into three epochs: first, Antiquity, in which men were terrorized by the forces of nature. Second, Christendom. Christ introduces the rule of the spirit, which destroys the fear of material things, but establishes the tyranny of the Idea. There is now a spook in every object. Third, the Unit, by the might of his own understanding and will, dismisses the spirits, the spooks; the rule of Ideas is broken. The Ego is not an abstract I. He is you, yourself, just as you are in flesh and blood, become simply sovereign, disdainful of all rule of Ideas, as Christ was of all rule of material powers.

Of the author's character as shown by his actions I will emphasize only one feature. He recognized in the woman the individual, as free as she cares to be, precisely as he did in the man. When we read of another German author as Stirner's disciple, who differs from him so radically in this, we may think that author somewhat of a plagiarist, perhaps, but certainly not a disciple, as alleged.

Others again are springing up to classify the Ego and Egoism in philosophy. The Ego of Stirner is—yourself, if you like. You, as a person of flesh and blood, will not be successfully classified

job." Indeed, sir, if you have a determination not to take it I am sure you will not take it—unless some stronger interest of yours comes into play. We will wait and see what you do. Professions are cheap.

in "philosophy," I think, if you grasp the idea and act on it. The old so-called philosophic Egoism was a disquisition on the common characteristics of men, a sort of generality. The real living Egoism is the fact of untrammeled mind in this or that person and the actions resulting, the end of the tyranny of general ideas.

BIOGRAPHICAL SKETCH OF JAMES L. WALKER

To write a just biographical sketch of a man who has completed the execution of life-long plans is hardly possible. To do justice at writing the life of a man who was cut off by death at the moment of attainment from the execution of plans that had been ripening for almost a lifetime, is quite impossible. In the first undertaking when concrete accomplishment is chronicled there is revealed at least an approximation of the reach and depth of thought exerted; and the failure to depict such a life task may be only in the matter of intensity. While in the second effort the failure must come in the very vital point of inability to reveal even the objects to be accomplished, to say nothing of the breadth reached, depth penetrated, and the infinite detail encompassed by the mind of a brain now numb and forever stilled.

The life work of James L. Walker presents this lamentable difficulty. This point can perhaps be no more forcefully illustrated than in the following editorial review of what was known of him and his life, published in the *News*, Galveston, Texas, Apr. 19, 1904, upon the receipt of the news of his death:

> "Through a letter received yesterday by Mr. Edwin Bruce, secretary of the Galveston school board, the *News* learns of the death of Dr. James L. Walker, which occurred at Lardo, Mexico, April 2, after an illness of sixteen days. Dr. Walker went to Mexico about seven years aga and was for a number of years connected with a newspaper at Monterey. The *News* understands that he studied medicine and practiced for some time when he was a young man, and after getting out of the newspaper business in Mexico he resumed practice as a physician. Mr. Walker was for many years connected with the editorial department of the *Galveston-Dallas News*. He was a deep thinker and a forcible writer. He had few intel-

lectual equals in the state. He belonged to the old school of solid writers, what the present generation call heavy. Those who knew him best recognized him as an intellectual giant. He was pre-eminently a logician and incidentally a fine linguist, versed in dead languages, and a fluent conversationalist in half a dozen modern tongues.

"Owing to his quiet mode of life, few knew of him personally. He was a man who had little to say about himself individually. This is demonstrated by the fact that while he was associated for a number of years with men now connected with the *News*, there is not one of his former associates who could state with definiteness as to his age or his nationality. Mr. Walker was always ready to discuss any topic of the day or any topic in history with the greatest fluency, but had little to say about his personal affairs. At the same time there was nothing about him to enable one to call him distant or say he was too reserved.

"After severing his connection with the *News* in 1895, he read law, and was admitted to the bar and practiced at Galveston a short time before he went to Mexico. Mr. Walker was a deep thinker, a ripe scholar and an elegant gentleman. He leaves a wife, who was with him at the time of his death."

The writer of this effort is handicapped by the same difficulty as was the editor of the *Galveston News*;—more appreciation for the subject than knowledge of his doings. Although there was maintained between Mr. Walker on the one hand, and Georgia Replogle and me on the other, quite a dozen years of correspondence of such a confidential nature as may readily exist between a fond master and his devoted disciples, and this was supplemented by some months of daily association, nevertheless not a sufficient number of facts concerning his past life were gathered to form even a tolerable biography. He talked, always apparently without reserve, about his past when it became incident to the conversation, and would doubtless have answered direct questions concerning it, but no one even dreamed of biography; he was so hale and hearty, and withal so careful of his health that he seemed easily good for more than a score of years. So the precious opportunity was lost in planning for the future rather than in reviewing the past, which would so much better have served this need.

Outside of Mr. Walker's work in the Liberal World, no biographical information has been obtained save this reproduction of another article written by a personal friend of his and published in the *Galveston News* the day following the publication of the above-quoted editorial:

> "The death of Dr. James L. Walker mentioned in today's *News*, causes sorrow here [Waco, Texas,] where the deceased had many friends.
>
> "Dr. Walker was born in June 1845, at Manchester, England, of wealthy parents, who gave him a liberal education. After graduating at institutions of learning in England, France, and Germany, he became connected with the *London Times*. On reaching the United States he became an associate editor on the *Chicago Times*. In Texas at various periods he worked editorially on the *San Antonia Herald*, the *San Antonio Express*, the *Galveston-Dallas News*, the *Austin Statesman*, the *State Gazette of Austin*, and other papers. He was the author of works on stenography, chemistry, medicine, and civil engineering. He had a reading and speaking acquaintance with ten living languages, and was proficient in Greek, Latin, and Sanskrit. In 1865 he was wedded to Katharine Smith, of Illinois, who survives him. After his marriage he came to Texas with his wife, and before returning to newspaper work he taught in colleges. He traveled all over both hemispheres."

Mr. Walker's name was properly, simply James Walker, the

initial "L" being adopted in the exigency of his mail matter becoming confused with that of other James Walkers in some of the various localities in which he lived. But as he was known as James L. Walker to the Liberal World, by whom these chapters will doubtless be first read and most appreciated, the name has been so written in this booklet.

It was incidentally learned in conversation with Mr. Walker that his Iconoclastic and Liberalizing work began very early in life, as he published in Chicago a 40-column anti-theological paper and debated and lectured on Sundays besides, for almost two years prior to his marriage and departure for Texas, which is said to have occurred in 1865. The paper was sustained principally by Freethinker merchants of the city; and although it gathered a considerable list of regular subscribers, the cold, damp lake climate afflicted Mr. Walker's lungs and throat so unfavorably that he abandoned the enterprise, and sought the drier air and milder temperature of the Southwest.

His next innovating work in the realm of Liberal thought was, as nearly as memory serves, some articles on "Conscience," contributed to *Lucifer*, at that time published at Valley Falls, Kansas. These articles, if memory again is correct, stirred up very bitter opposition from some of the more emotionalistic readers of that journal; but they also carried off several valuable adherents to the ideas presented.

Again, in the years 1886-7, Mr. Walker, over the *nom de plume* "Tak Kak," made his most widely effective effort in the propaganda of the new ethics by means of some articles on the "Duty" idea, in *Liberty*, the pioneer organ of Philosophical Anarchism, then published in Boston, Mass. Here, once more, most bitter opposition was aroused, practically dividing the Anarchistic camp; but he firmly established the Egoistic idea, and carried with him almost all the readers of that journal, as well as its editor. Among those who from reading this discussion were led to embrace the Egoistic philosophy, were the projectors and publishers of the little magazine "Egoism," through which the publication of these chapters was inaugurated.

In the above-indicated memorable discussion in *Liberty*, Mr. Walker won the distinctive title of "Father of Egoism in America." Although Dr. Caspar Schmidt, a comparatively unknown author, had under the nom de plume "Max Stirner," previously written a masterly and inimitable work in Germany on the philosophy, Mr. Walker had thought out and systemized the same in this country before he heard of Stirner. As a result of this discussion in *Liberty*, a distinctive and widely distributed school of the greatest solidarity has sprung into existence, and includes among its adherents the brightest and ablest ethical polemics of our time.

In this discussion or incident to it, Mr. Walker, in pointing out that Anarchism is really only the political branch of Egoism proper, also earned credit for suggesting the genealogical and consistently descriptive name. Egoistic Anarchism, for the Anarchism hitherto designated as Philosophical Anarchism, to distinguish its school from that of the physical force revolutionists who also claim to be Anarchists.

Mr. Walker's next and last effort in sociological writing was the chapters herein contained. This was to be followed by a treatise on Liberty;—liberty to try expedients for bettering our condition. There was then to be one on Money—an exchange medium; and another on Land—the right to produce a living; and finally, Suggestions on Colonizing. He entertained, of course, the same cosmopolitan economic ideas that are held by all of the Anarchistic school, but he believed that under present conditions of waiting for education to soak into the masses, and as an educator itself, colonization was highly desirable. One plan was to colonize in cities, in a given section if convenient, and to strive to achieve economic independence by at first diverting patronage to the members of the colony, and finally thus establishing mutual industrial hold in the community at large. The other plan was to locate on the land in large bodies and to organize industry also on a purely voluntary basis; the main idea being aggregation of people of similar views, thus eliminating as far as possible the authoritarian interference of Philistine political polity.

Besides these projected sociological works, Mr. Walker had put into manuscript, several years before his death, two educational works. The nature of the one has slipped the memory altogether; the other was a system of Spanish shorthand. But owing to the indifference of Spanish-speaking peoples toward modern methods in producing their literature, its publication was abandoned for the time.

Mr. Walker may have had other works on other subjects in contemplation, but these were all that were learned of in the incidental manner in which all that is here written was obtained. He was also interested in telepathy, and in hygienic matters, but nothing was mentioned of a treatise on either subject.

During the years that Mr. Walker was editorially connected with the *Galveston News*, he continuously wrote masterly and powerful articles concerning the various political issues as they passed. These were the dread of all contemporaries, as none could gainsay his arguments, based as they were on the incontrovertible principles of his philosophy. And it may be added that the *Galveston News* was everywhere the delight and pride of the school he represented, it being the only daily paper in the world enunciating any sound economic and political doctrines. But in time there came an end to all this. Finally someone learned the basis of these impregnable positions and informed contemporary papers, which being unable to answer the arguments, started the mad-dog cry, "Anarchy." So, whatever may have been the inclination of the *News* management, the result was that Mr. Walker was reduced to the merely mechanical function of correcting for the compositors, copy that had been written by others.

After continuing in this menial position for three years, inducements were held out by certain wealthy Mexicans and resident Americans to come to Monterey, Mexico, and establish a Spanish-English daily newspaper. But by the time Mr. Walker could arrive on the ground, the enthusiasm of these same persons had become so limp that he abandoned the enterprise. Thereupon he started an English weekly paper for the patronage of the American colony numbering about 2,000 persons. And, although operating in a country in which every editor is directly responsible to the government for every word by him published, he created a local paper which in its scope and penetration of subjects handled was probably never equaled in any country. This he published for several years, but publications cut no figure with Mexicans, and Americans located in Mexico soon become Mexicanized and equally disinterested. Therefore he dropped publication, and entered upon the practice of medicine, having been licensed to practice years before in Texas.

In the year 1902, Mr. Walker and his wife came to Denver to spend the hot season away from Mexico. It was upon this occasion that the writer was favored with the personal acquaintance of this man whom he learned to reverence and love more than any other man he ever met. And, when the annulling blow of life fell, he would have fled to the arms of this fatherly and brotherly master, even as the dismayed child flees to its mother; but alas, fate had carefully destroyed the balm many days before she laid agape the wound.

In the latter part of that year Mr. Walker returned to Mexico to dispose of his effects there, then to visit the St. Louis exposition in 1904, and from there to locate somewhere in the United States. The disposal of his effects had been accomplished, and he was about to leave Mexico, when he was overtaken by the inevitable monster. He had passed through the yellow fever epidemic in Monterey that year, but not without being attacked. However, he succeeded in breaking the fever, and had so far recovered as to be about to return to the United States preparatory to carrying out his original plans, when he changed his mind, believing it better to travel with his wife in the interior of Mexico, pursuant of some business there until the weather should be warmer at the North. He was still weak from the depletion of the fever when unfortunately he and his wife ran unwarned into epidemic smallpox. They fled immediately to a back town, hoping to escape the contagion, but all in vain; it had already fastened upon the weakened man. And although Mr. Walker was himself an Allopathic practitioner*, and therefore more or less committed to heroic methods of treatment, he knew so well the ideas and practice of Mexican doctors that he feared their medication more than the disease. So the next effort was an attempt to conceal his condition, in order to evade the rigorous medication of the authorities. But this also failed, and this precious man was seized by Mexican officials and carried to a native "hospital;" and, of course, doped to his death with the regulation life-extinguisher of the authoritarian State that he had fought with his most powerful ammunition during most of the best years of his life.

He had succeeded in pulling himself through a much more severe malady in the instance of the yellow fever attack, when he was in his own home and amid acquaintanceship that allowed him his own medical resources. And, he probably would have succeeded again with this less malignant affliction if he had not been subjected to the excitement of seizure at a critical stage of the affection and thereafter to the iron-clad usage of a prisoner.

His wife was permitted to remain by his side and do all that might be done, but unfortunately this did not include kicking

* *Allopathic* normally refers, derogatorily, to mainstream medicine by practitioners of Homeopathy. [ed.]

out the Mexican doctor with his regulation decoctions that the delicate constitution of the victim could not combat. He suffered great agony and was delirious much of the time; recovering consciousness, however, a few hours before his death clearly enough to realize the situation, for calling his wife to him, he said: "We can't overcome this." And thus she was left to part alone from this immeasurable soul in that barbaric land;—even forced to leave all that was left to her of him, lying in the midst of the wretched beasts whose sloven lives had poisoned away the adored being who meant all to her that existence meant.

The grave was protected against the Mexican habit of burying over the same ground again and again, by deeply-laid concrete surmounted by a strong iron enclosure embedded in this concrete. According to Mexican law the remains, after five years burial, may be removed. This will probably be done by the devoted wife.

It is said above that Mrs. Walker was left to "part alone," etc. Figuratively, this is true; literally, not. There happened to be one American in a nearby town who, fortunately, was an acquaintance, and being summoned at the last, aided so far as lay in his power to the end of this calamitous tragedy.

Mr. Walker was an ideal Egoist. While he taught the doctrines of equity wherever the subject was seasonable, (and the humblest novice could be no more ready at all times than he to do a full share in associative effort with his own kind); nevertheless he permitted the Philistine World to pay him all the homage and tribute it cared to. He sacrificed none of his strength promiscuously upon the altar of equality to the unappreciative unequal,—as is the wont of the evangelistic enthusiast. Toward earnest persons of his own general social ideal, he might "overflow," as he has so aptly, forcefully, and yet incidentally put in an early chapter, but always with an eye to a rational limit;—one which in his own mind, incurred no obligation on the part of the person thus favored. It was his idea that in co-operative effort, the directors of work, or "bosses," should not generally receive greater compensation than the manual workers in the same line, since the opportunities for relaxation would compensate them for the greater value of their services rendered to the body at large.

In association Mr. Walker was of the most lovable of men; calm, courteous, profound, and yet humorous upon occasion, but never light. In conversation, every proposition was an appeal to reason; there was no cramming of the assumptions of authority down the mental throat. He was as spontaneously in touch with the spirit of the occasion in the hovel, as with that in the drawing-room. He regarded the varying conditions of the rich man and the poor man with that same consideration which unlike neighbors might each elicit from him. He made no wry faces at the inconveniences of the poor, nor did he fawn over the luxury of the rich. Neither was there fanatical rebuke manifested against the commander of opulence. He elucidated at as great length and with the same interest to the one as to the other. What he imparted, or what he gave, was given with the air of a prince. There was none of the awful griping that is evinced by the Moralist when he does one of his "Duty" stunts, which seems to have cost him more than it ever could be worth to any other person.

In bearing Mr. Walker was dignified without a suggestion of austerity, or of snobbishness. Tall, and erect in carriage, muscular and athletic, he was sure to attract that attention which melts into admiration. His language, while absolutely correct, flowed without a tinge of the strain of pedagogic discipline so conspicuous in the conversation of the majority of "educated" people. All who enjoyed his confidence and won his interest must over regret that the pleasant hours of relaxation and conversation are never to be repeated.

Never shall I forget the last evening spent with this genuinely great unknown. He came out to my bleak little suburban home, where we spent the evening alone, and under the stimulus of the parting occasion and all the final things being felt and said, he seemed more magnificent than ever in his imperial democracy and embracing comradeship. It was a balmy night with the clearest of Colorado's clear skies and the brightest of her moonlight, and as we sat in the still open, the homogeneity of the scene;— the great sky, the vast plain, and the great man, fairly assaulted even my usually pre-occupied senses.

It was Mr. Walker's purpose to accumulate at least a moderately independent fortune, before launching into a considerable effort of sociological and other innovating writings. This part of his program was fairly well accomplished, when the Galveston flood came, obliterating much of his holdings altogether; there being a considerable portion of it at the bottom of the sea when the tidal wave subsided. So he probably would have devoted at least a few more years to repairing so far as possible the breach in his fortune, before uncovering his light to the world of dungeoned mentality. But, alas!.....................*

—Henry Replogle

---

* This sketch should, fittingly, have been written by Benjamin R. Tucker, previously referred to as the editor of *Liberty*. Mr. Walker had no warmer friend or greater admirer than Mr. Tucker, who possesses in addition, the advantages of scholarship and literary training, so necessary in comprehensively and lucidly celebrating so worthy a subject. But Mr. Tucker was abroad, and the date of his probable return unknown. Moreover, the publication of the booklet at this time seemed very urgent, inasmuch as the details of the work were in such a shape that no one besides me could well perform the task. My health, also, was in such a precarious condition that life itself was unusually uncertain. For this reason Mrs. Walker was naturally very anxious to complete the work while it was still possible. So I undertook the sketch myself, hoping to redeem it in a future edition with one written by the proper person. This one has been written between rounds of oiling and inspection, while on duty in the engine-room of a steam plant, and without access to any data save those supplied by memory, possibly badly blurred by psychical prostration. The whole was then corrected to approximately the present shape by the kindly aid of some friends.

TESTIMONY OF THE APOSTLES OF EGOISM

Know thyself.

—Solon.

Knowledge is power.

—Bacon.

To thine own self be true.

—Shakespeare.

The beautiful is always severe.

—Ségur.

If it be right to me, it is right.

—Stirner.

Moderation is the pleasure of the wise.

—Voltaire

God helps them [only] who help themselves.

—Franklin.

Love is the union of a want and a sentiment.

—Lamartine.

Self-love is not so vile a sin as self-neglecting.

—Shakespeare.

To scoff at philosophy is to act as a true philosopher.

—Pascal.

Every mortal is relieved by speaking of his misfortunes.

—*Chénier.*

Man is Creation's master-piece. But who says so?—Man.

—*Gavarni.*

It is difficult to free fools from the chains they revere.

—*Voltaire.*

He who is devoted to everybody is devoted to nobody.

—*Delavigne.*

God is generally on the side of the strongest battalions.

—*Napoleon.*

Under the freest constitution ignorant people are still slaves.

—*Condorcet.*

In jealousy there is usually more self-love than love.

—*Rochefoucauld.*

Goodness, for the most part, is but indolence, or impotence.

—*Ibid.*

When our vices leave us, we flatter ourselves we are leaving them.

—*Ibid.*

The greatest of all pleasures is to give pleasure to one we love.

—*Boufflers.*

We like those to whom we do good better than those who do us good.

—*Saint-Réal.*

Trust in God and [that is, so far as you] keep your powder dry.

—*Cromwell.*

It is easier to be good for everybody, than to be good for somebody.

—*A. Dumas, fils.*

The more honest a man is, the less he affects the airs of a saint.

—*Lavater.*

To know man, borrow the ear of the blind and the eye of the deaf.

—*Ibid.*

Who despises all that is despicable, is made to be impressed with all that is grand.

—*Ibid.*

Everybody exclaims against ingratitude. Are there so many benefactors?

—*Bougeart.*

A woman by whom we are loved is a vanity; a woman whom we love is a religion.

—*Giradin.*

Diversity of opinion proves that things are only what we think them.

—*Montaigne.*

To love is to ask of another the happiness that is lacking in ourselves.

—*Rochepedre.*

Virtue is so praiseworthy that wicked people practice it from self-interest.

—*Vauvenargues.*

There is pleasure in meeting the eyes of those to whom we have done good.

—*La Bruyère.*

The art of conversation consists less in showing one's own wit than in giving opportunity for the display of the wit of others.

—*Ibid.*

Egoism is another name for self-preservation; the egoist, after providing for self, turns altruist.

—*Tilden.*

High positions are like the summit of high, steep rocks: eagles and reptiles alone can reach them.

—*Mme. Necker.*

The men of future generations will yet win many a liberty of which we do not even feel the want.

—*Stirner.*

One is free in proportion as one is strong; there is no real liberty save that which one takes for one's self.

—*Ib.*

There are persons who do not know how to waste their time alone and hence become the scourge of busy people.

—*Bonald.*

Not to enjoy one's youth when one is young, is to imitate the miser who starves beside his treasures.

—Mme. Louise Colet.

All passions are good when one masters them; all are bad when one is a slave to them. [The same is true of ideas].

—Rousseau.

You can tell more about a man's character by trading horses with him once than you can by hearing him talk for a year in prayer meeting.

—American Maxim.

Forget this superstition [that the day of noble deeds is past], steep your souls in Plutarch, and through believing in his heroes, dare to believe in yourselves.

—Nietzsche.

To be regardful of others within reason is intelligent egoism, but it is necessary to distinguish those who are worthy of our regard from those who are not.

—Tak Kak.

The discoverer of a great truth well knows that it may be useful to other men, and, as a greedy with-holding would bring him no enjoyment, he communicates it.

—Stirner.

Everywhere the strong have made the laws and oppressed the weak, and, if they have sometimes consulted the interests of society, they have always forgotten those of humanity.

—Turgot.

Napoleon the exploiter said, "The heart of a statesman should be in his head." The exploited will never be saved till they make the brain the seat of their patriotic affections.

Religion and moralism say that we may have passions, but we must not allow our passions to enslave us. The egoist extends the suggestion to include ideas. He has ideas, but he remains the master of them. All the ideas he has he will use as he sees fit. If of a speculative intellectual turn, the egoist cannot doubt that there is the greatest good for all in egoism, and as he can find satisfaction in proving it, he may undertake to do so.

—*Tak Kak.*

EGOISM AS TAUGHT BY THOREAU

Thoreau had watched [Human] Nature like a detective who is to go upon the stand.

—Lowell.

Cease to gnaw that crust. There is ripe fruit over your head.

—Summer.

This life is not for complaint but for satisfaction.

—Letter.

To reject religion is the first step towards moral excellence.

—Essay.

The whole duty of man may be expressed in one line: Make to yourself a perfect body.

—Summer.

All the world is forward to prompt him who gets up to live without his creed in his pocket.

—Week.

In what concerns you much, do not think that you have companions : know that you are alone in the world.

—Letter.

I have enjoyed very much my visits to you . . . but life is short and there are also other things to be done.

—Letter.

There is no more fatal blunderer than he who consumes the greater part of his life getting his living.

—Life without Principle.

If there is an experiment which you would like to try, try it. Do not entertain doubts if they are not agreeable to you.

—Letter.

Do not be too moral. You may cheat yourself out of much life so. Aim above morality. Be not simply good; be good for something.

—Letter.

The wisest man preaches no doctrines; he has no scheme; he sees no rafter, not even a cobweb against the heavens. It is clear sky.

— Week.

He is the true artist whose life is his material. Every stroke of the chisel must enter his own flesh and bones and not grate dully on marble.

—Summer.

The man who goes alone can start today; but he who travels with another must wait till that other is ready, and it may be a long time before they get off.

—Walden.

There is something servile in the habit of seeking after a law which we may obey. We may study the laws of matter at and for our convenience, but a successful life knows no law.

—Walking.

If you would travel farther than all travellers, be naturalized in all climes, and cause the Sphinx to dash her head against a stone, ever obey the precept of the old philosopher and explore thyself.

—Walden.

Warm your body by healthful exercise, not by cowering over a stove. Warm your spirit by performing independently noble deeds, not by ignobly seeking the sympathy of your fellows who are no better than yourself.

—Chastity and Sensuality.

The philanthropist too often surrounds mankind with the remembrance of his own cast-off griefs as an atmosphere, and calls it sympathy. We should impart our courage, and not our disease, and take care that this does not spread by contagion.

—Walden.

In proportion as our inward life fails, we go more constantly and desperately to the post office. You may depend on it, that the poor fellow who walks away with the greatest number of letters, proud of his extensive correspondence, has not heard from himself this long while.

—Life without Principle.

VIA HELLOROSA

Scenes on the Way to Hades

The Engines of Hell running full blast, day and night.
Watchman what of the night? And the Watchman said,
"I see a great light—in fact, I see the flames of Hell."

One cannot bring the masses to shout hosanna until one rides into the city on an ass.

—Nietzsche.

Between the government which does evil and the people who accept it—there is a certain shameful solidarity.

—Victor Hugo.

Within the memory of man the trade of governing has always been monopolized by the most ignorant and most rascally individuals of mankind.

—Thomas Paine.

We shall have an Emperor in Washington within 25 years unless we can create a public sentiment which, regardless of legislation, will regulate the trusts.

—A. T. Hadley, Pres. of Yale College.

We have among us people who would like to abolish radically everything that exists and carry us back, by violence if need be, to a régime discarded and condemned more than a century ago. They are called conservatives.

—Paul Masson.

With the development of capitalistic production, European public opinion has stripped the last rag off conscience and modesty. Each nation glories cynically in all the infamy that goes to hasten the accumulation of capital.

—Flaubert.

This old society has long since been judged and condemned. Let justice be done! Let this old world be broken into pieces! ...where innocence has perished, where villany has prospered, where man is exploited by man! Let these whited sepulchres, full of lying and iniquity, be utterly destroyed!

—Heine.

We say that your society is not even a society, that it is not even the shadow of one, but an assemblage of persons that can be given no name: administered, manipulated, exploited at the will of your caprices, a warren, a flock, a herd of human cattle destined by you to glut your greed.

—Lamennais.

What kind of society is it which, at this period, has, for its base, inequality and injustice? Would it not be well to take the whole by the four corners and send it pell-mell up to the ceiling, the cloth, the feast, and the orgy, the gluttony and the drunkenness and the guests; those who have their two elbows on the table, and those who are on all fours under it, to spew the whole lot in God's face and to fling the whole world at heaven? The hell of the poor makes the paradise of the rich. Not only has happiness not come, but honour has fled.

— Victor Hugo.

Imperialism is a depraved choice of national life, imposed by self-seeking interests which appeal to the lusts of acquisitiveness and of dominion surviving in a nation from centuries of animal struggle for existence. Its adoption as a policy implies a deliberate renunciation of that cultivation of the higher inner qualities which for a nation, as for an individual, constitutes the ascendancy of reason over brute impulse. It is the besetting sin of all successful states, and its penalty is unalterable- in the order of nature.

—*J. A. Hobson's* Imperialism.

THE EAGLE & THE SERPENT

Time cannot bend the line which Truth hath writ. The passion for destruction is a creative passion.

—Bakounine.

In Hobbes' system morality is the rationalization of egoism. Justice is a ruse of the weak to defend themselves.

—Nietzsche.

We can only be valued as we make ourselves valuable.

—Emerson.

The indisputableness of eternal injustice is a part of Nietzsche's system. One must read all moralists with an eye to their motives.

—Nietzsche.

He who tells the truth is turned out of nine cities.

—Turkish Proverb.

Justice is an "equilibrium of might," non-existent for the absolutely powerless.

—Nietzsche.

Government has nothing to give me except that which it takes from me.

—A. Bellegarigue.

Conscience and remorse are the results of our blindness to the real origin of the sentiments called moral

—Nietzsche.

Are not all tragedies due to the fact that people do not die at the right time?

—John Erwin McCall.

He's a slave who cannot be in the right without two or three—just by "his own self."

—John Erwin McCall.

Ascetic Ideals.—Ideals should always be fictitious. When they become real they cease to be ideal. All extremes are wrong.

—John Erwin McCall.

Journalism is the art of selling to other people their own prejudices and false opinions at the highest possible price.

—John Erwin McCall.

Benevolence is as purely selfish as greed. No one would do a benevolent action if he thought it would entail remorse.

—Dod Grile. (Ambrose Bierce)

Origin of Optimism.—The typical optimist sits in the British Museum, which was built by money stolen from the Spanish, and which the Spanish had stolen from the Aztecs, and piously exclaims, "A good to one is a good to all."

—John Erwin McCall.

WISDOM & WICKEDNESS OF LA ROCHEFOUCAULD

When love increases, prudence decreases.

Our virtues are commonly disguised vices.

Fortune and caprice govern the world.

Judgment is only the perfection of wit.

Self-love is the greatest of flatterers.

Men are oftener treacherous through weakness than design.

We never ardently desire what we desire rationally.

We forgive just as long as we love.

Hypocrisy is the homage that vice pays to virtue.

Human prudence rightly understood is circumspect enlightened self-love.

We seldom heartily praise those who do not admire us.

We easily forget crimes that are known only to ourselves.

Whatever good is said of us we learn nothing new.

To study man is more necessary than to study books.

We please oftener by our defects than by our virtues.

The greatest miracle in love is that it cures coquetry.

There are reproaches which praise and there are praises which reproach.

In jealousy there is less of love than of self-love.

To live without envy is a certain indication of great qualities.

The virtues and vices are all put in motion by interest.

Self-love is more artful than the most artful of men.

It is a sort of coquetry to boast that we never coquet.

It is our own vanity that makes the vanity of others intolerable.

We promise according to our hopes and perform according to our fears.

The virtue of women is often the love of reputation and quiet.

The misfortunes of other people we all bear with heroic constancy.

Gravity is a stratagem invented to conceal the poverty of the mind.

An extraordinary haste to discharge an obligation it a sort of ingratitude.

Envy is destroyed by true friendship as coquetry is by true love.

We should have but little pleasure were we never to flatter ourselves.

We should be above jealousy when there is real cause for it.

The virtues are lost in self-interest as rivers are lost in the sea.

When our vices leave us, we flatter ourselves that we have left them.

A resolution never to deceive others, exposes a man to be deceived, himself.

Were we perfectly acquainted with our idol we should never passionately desire it.

Did we not flatter ourselves, the flattery of others could never hurt us.

Flattery is a sort of bad money to which our vanity gives currency.

Interest speaks all languages, and acts all parts, even that of *disinterestedness* itself.

The more you love your mistress the readier you are to hate her.

We confess small faults, in order to insinuate that we have no great ones.

Magnanimity is the good sense of pride; and the noblest way of acquiring applause.

To be great, we must know how to push our fortune to the utmost.

The gratitude of most men is only a secret desire to receive greater favours.

Small geniuses are hurt by small events; great geniuses see through and despise them.

The man who thinks he loves his mistress for *her* sake is much mistaken.

Men sometimes think they hate flattery, whilst they hate only the manner of it.

A woman often thinks she regrets the lover when she only regrets the love.

Old age gives good advice when it is no longer able to give bad example.

To praise great actions with sincerity, may be said, to be taking part in them.

Self-love, as it happens to be well or ill-conducted, constitutes virtue or vice.

Men would not live long in society, were they not the mutual dupes of each other.

It is less dangerous to do ill to most men than to do them much good.

You seldom find people ungrateful so long as you are in a condition to serve them.

In the distress of our best friends we always find something that does not displease us.

A man of wit would often be at a loss, were it not for the company of fools.

To judge of love by most of its effects, one would think it more like hatred than kindness.

We are much nearer loving those who hate us, than those who love us more thaw we like.

We despise not all those who have vices; yet we despise all those who have no virtues.

We are far happier when deceived by those we are in love with than when undeceived.

Nothing is more natural or more fallacious than to persuade ourselves that we are beloved.

Philosophy easily triumphs over past and future ills; but *present* ills triumph over philosophy.

Absence destroys small passions and increases great ones the wind extinguishes tapers but kindles fires.

The modesty which seems to decline praise is the desire of being praised with more delicacy.

The reason why lovers never weary of each other's company is because they speak always of themselves.

Before we passionately desire anything which another enjoys we should examine into the happiness of its possessor.

We should often be ashamed of our best actions if the world saw the motives which inspire us.

We are so used to disguise ourselves to others that at last we become disguised even to ourselves.

To the honour of virtue it must be acknowledged, that the greatest misfortunes befall men from their vices.

Our enemies, in their judgment of us, come nearer to truth than we do ourselves. [The Golden Rule.]

It is not always from the principle of valor and chastity that men are valiant, or women are chaste.

Notwithstanding all the discoveries that have been made in the regions of self-love, there still remains much *terra incognita*.

Perfect valor consists in doing without a witness all that we should be capable of doing before all the world.

Love, like fire, cannot subsist without continual motion; as soon as it ceases to hope or fear, it ceases to exist.

What seems generosity is often no more than disguised ambition; which overlooks a small pleasure in order to gratify a great one.

None deserve the character of being good, who have not spirit enough to be bad; goodness, for the most part, is either indolence or impotence.

To be deceived by our enemies, or betrayed by our friends, is insupportable; yet are we often content to be so served by ourselves.

Jealousy is, in some sort, rational and just ; it aims at the preservation of that which belongs, or which we fancy belongs to us.

Since great men cannot bestow either health of body, or peace of mind, we certainly pay too dear for all that they can bestow.

In our concern for the misfortunes of our enemies there is often more pride than goodness of heart. By showing our compassion we make them feel our superiority.

We are so prepossessed in our favour that we often mistake for virtues those vices that bear some resemblance to them, and which are artfully disguised by self-love.

Self-love never reigns so absolutely as in the passion of love; we are always ready to sacrifice the peace of those we adore, rather than lose the least part of our own.

Everybody takes pleasure in returning small obligations; many go so far as to acknowledge moderate ones; but there is hardly anyone who does not repay great obligations with ingratitude.

We love everything on our own account; we even follow our own taste and inclination when we prefer our friends to ourselves; and yet it is this preference alone that constitutes true and perfect friendship.

The love of glory, the fear of shame, the design of making a fortune, the desire of rendering life easy and agreeable, and the humour of pulling down other people, are often the causes of that valor so celebrated among men.

WISDOM & WICKEDNESS OF CHAMFORT

To despise money is to dethrone a king.

The beginning of wisdom is the fear of man.

The world either breaks or hardens the heart.

He who has no character is not a man—he is a thing.

Love—agreeable foolery: ambition—serious stupidity.

The loves of some peoples are but the result of good suppers.

Prejudice, vanity, calculation; these are what govern the world.

The public! the public! How many fools does it take to make a public?

In politics and in gallantry really wise men do not fight for conquests.

Enjoy and give enjoyment, without injury to thyself or to others; this is true morality.

Intelligent people make many blunders because they never believe the world as stupid as it is.

Love pleases more than marriage for the reason that romance is more interesting than history.

You run the risk of being disgusted if you pry into the processes of cookery, government, or justice.

A man in deep mourning is asked: "Good God! whom have you lost?" "I?" says he, "I have lost nothing, I am a widower."

We have three kinds of friends; those who love us, those who are indifferent to us and those who hate us.

The best philosophy to employ towards the world is to alloy the sarcasm of gaiety with the indulgence of contempt.

In love all is true and all is false. It is the only thing on which you cannot possibly say an absurdity.

The ambitious one who failed in his aim and lives in despair reminds me of Ixion broken on the wheel for having embraced a cloud.

An Englishman condemned to be hanged received the King's pardon. "The law's on my side," he protested, "they shall hang me!"

Our happiness depends upon a multitude of circumstances which do not manifest themselves, which one does not, and can not speak of.

We may wager that any idea of the public, or any general opinion, is a folly since it has received the approbation of a majority of the people.

"The difference between you and me," said a philosopher, "is that you say to masked hypocrites 'I know you' while I leave them to think that they have deceived me."

Someone asked a child "Is God the Father, God?" "Yes."—"And God the Son, is He God?" "Not yet, that I know of; but on the death of His father He cannot fail to come into the succession."

Mr. L. to turn Mrs. B. (for long a widow) from the idea of marrying, said to her "Don't you see, it's a grand thing to bear the name of a man who can commit no more stupidities."

Hope is but a quack who cheats us continually and I for one felt happy when I had lost my hopes. I should put on the gates of Paradise the words which Dante put over the entrance to Hell: *Abandon hope, all ye who enter here.*

The physical world appears to be the work of a powerful and good being, who has been obliged to leave the execution of a part of his scheme to a demon; but the moral world seems to be the product of the whims of a demon gone mad.

Milton after the restoration of Charles II was on the way to securing again a lucrative office which he had lost. His wife urged him. He replied: "You are a woman, and you want a coach; as for me, I want to live and die an honest man."

Someone told M. "You are very fond of consideration." He replied in a way that struck me: "No, I have consideration for myself and that sometimes secures me the consideration of others."

A bright woman told me once that when choosing a sweetheart a woman pays more regard to what other women say about the man of her choice than to her own opinion of him.

One must be able to combine the contraries: love of virtue with indifference for public opinion: taste for work with indifference for glory: the care of one's health with indifference for life.

When one has been tormented and fatigued by his sensitiveness, he learns that be must live from day to day, forget all that is possible, and efface his life from memory as it passes.

A man passed all his evenings for 30 years with a lady other than his wife. He finally lost his wife; one believed be would marry the other, and recommended him to do so. He refused. "I should not know," said he "where to go to pass my evenings."

I asked R., a man full of wit and talent, why he had shown himself so little in the revolution of 1789. He replied: "It was because, for 30 years, I had found men so wicked privately and individually, that I did not dare to hope any good of them in public and taken collectively."

A young man asked me why Mrs. B. had refused the homage he offered, to run after Mr. L. who seemed to refuse her advances. I told him: "My dear friend, Genoa, rich and powerful, offered its sovereignty to several kings, who all refused it; yet they went to war to possess Corsica, which produces nothing except chestnuts, but which was proud and independent."

Rousseau, it is said, had been favoured by the Countess of Boufflers, and had even gone so far as to neglect her, which put them in a bad temper with one another. One day someone remarked in their presence that the love of the human race extinguishes love of country. "For my part," said she, "I judge by myself and I feel it is not true. I am a very good Frenchwoman, and I none the less interest myself in the happiness of all." "Yes, I understand you," said Rousseau, "you are French at heart, and cosmopolitan as regards the rest of your person."

FLASHES OF LIGHTNING FROM NIETZSCHE

I write no longer with words but with flashes of lightning.

–Nietzsche

Nietzsche is the Pascal of Paganism.

—Dr. Havelock Ellis' Affirmations.

Our old morality is a piece of comedy.

—The Genealogy of Morals.

Help thyself: then every one else helps thee. Principle of brotherly love. In order that a sanctuary may be erected, a sanctuary must be broken down.

—The Genealogy of Morals.

To rear an animal which may promise—is not this the true problem of man?

—The Genealogy of Morals.

The sickly are the great danger of man: not the evil, not the "beasts of prey."

—The Genealogy of Morals.

Not through wrath but through laughter one slayeth. Arise let us slay the spirit of gravity.

—Zarathustra.

We modern men are the heirs of millenniums of conscience-vivisection and animal self-torture.

—The Genealogy of Morals.

With its contempt for the body Christianity was the greatest misfortune that ever befell humanity.

We have never sought for ourselves—how, then, could it happen, that some day we should find ourselves?

—*The Genealogy of Morals.*

The most malignant conspiracy is the conspiracy of the sufferers against the well-constituted.

—*The Genealogy of Morals.*

Whosoever will be free, must make himself free: freedom is no fairy's gift to fall into any man's lap.

The happy alone are the pledges of the future; they alone lie under an obligation for the future of man.

—*The Genealogy of Morals.*

Nietzsche regards Schopenhauer as the leader from Kant's caves of critical scepticism to the open sky with its consoling stars.

—*Dr. Havelock Ellis' Affirmations.*

"Rome against Judea, Judea against Rome."—So far no greater event has occurred than this struggle, this question, this deadly inimical antithesis.

—*The Genealogy of Morals.*

We must sacrifice all desirableness to truth, to each truth, even simple, bitter, ugly repulsive, unchristian, immoral truth...For there are such truths.

—*Dr. Havelock Ellis' Affirmations.*

In attacking the excessive tendency to sympathy which he seemed to see around him, Nietzsche was hygienically defending himself from his own excessive sympathy.

—*Dr. Havelock Ellis' Affirmations.*

The philosopher avoids three showy and noisy things,—glory, princes and women; whereby it is not meant to be said, however, that they should not come to him.

—*The Genealogy of Morals.*

The theatre and music are the hashish and betel of Europeans, and the history of the so-called higher culture is largely the history of narcotics.

—*The Joyful Science.*

He could not take up the Imitation of Christ—the very word "imitation" being, as indeed Michelet had said before, the whole of Christianity—without physical repugnance.

— *Dr. Havelock Ellis' Affirmations.*

The artist only reaches the last summit of his greatness when he learns to see himself and his art below him, when he knows how to laugh at himself.

—*The Genealogy of Morals.*

There could not possibly have been a greater or more calamitous misunderstanding, than when the happy, the well-constituted, the powerful in body and soul, began to be doubtful about their right to happiness.

—*The Genealogy of Morals.*

Christianity [according to Nietzsche] was born of the decay of antiquity, and an the degenerate people of that time, it worked like a soothing balm ; their eyes and ears were sealed by age and they could no longer understand Epicurus and Epictetus.

—*Dr. Havelock Ellis' Affirmations.*

Nietszche names six French writers—Montaigne, La Rochefoucauld, La Bruyère, Fontenelle, Vanvenarges, Chamfort—who bring us nearer to Greek antiquity than any other group of modern authors, and contain more real thought than all the books of the German philosophers put together.

—Dr. Havelock Ellis' Affirmations.

Verily it will one day be my death that I choke with laughter, when seeing asses drunken, and hearing night watchmen thus doubt God. For all the old Gods came to an end long ago. And verily it was a good and joyful end of the Gods. They laughed themselves unto death.

—Zarathustra.

These views might be regarded as "lax" as predisposing to easy self-indulgence. Nietszche would have smiled at such a notion. Not yielding but mastering, was the key to his personal morality. "Every day is badly spent," Nietszche said, "in which a man has not once denied himself; this gymnastic is inevitable if a man will retain the joy of being his own master," The four cardinal virtues, as Nietzsche understood morals, are sincerity, courage, generosity and courtesy.

—Dr. Havelock Ellis' Affirmations.

Every animal, and hence also *La Béte Philosophe*, instinctively strives for an optimum of favorable conditions under which it is free to discharge fully its power and attains its maximum consciousness of power; every animal, quite as instinctively and with a keenness of scent which passes all understanding abhors every kind of disturber or obstacle which obstructs or could obstruct his road to the optimum (it is not its road to "happiness" of which I am now speaking, but its road to power, to action, to mightiest action, and actually, in most cases, its road to unhappiness).

—The Genealogy of Morals.

Modern morality, Nietzsche said, is founded on an extravagant dread of pain—in ourselves primarily, secondarily in others. Sympathy is fellow-suffering; to love one's neighbor as oneself is to dread his pain as we dread our own pain. The religion of love is built upon the fear of pain... Both the sympathetic man and the unsympathetic man, Nietzsche argues, are egoists. But the unsympathetic man is held to be a more admirable kind of egoist. It is best to win the strength that comes of experience and suffering—and to allow others also to play their own cards and win the same strength—shedding our tears in private and abhorring soft-heartedness as the foe of all manhood and courage. To call the unsympathetic man "wicked" and the sympathetic man "good" seemed to Nietzsche a fashion in morals, a fashion which will have its day. He believed he was the first to point out the danger of the prevailing fashion as a sort of moral impressionism, the outcome of hyperaesthesia peculiar to periods of decadence. Not indeed that Christianity is, or could be, carried out among us to its fullest extent—"that indeed would be a serious matter. If we were ever to become the object to others of the same stupidities and importunities which they expend on themselves, we should flee wildly as soon as we saw our neighbor approach and curse sympathy as heartily as we now curse egoism." Our deepest and most personal griefs, Nietzsche remarks elsewhere, remain unrevealed and incomprehensible to nearly all other persons, even to the "neighbor" who eats out of the same dish with us. And even though my grief should become visible, the dear sympathetic neighbor can know nothing of its complexity and results, of the organic economy of my soul. That my grief may be bound up with my happiness troubles him little. The devotee of the "religion of pity" will heal my sorrows without a moment's delay; he knows not that the way to my heaven must lie through my own hell, that happiness and unhappiness are twin sisters who grow up together or remain stunted together.

—Dr. Havelock Ellis' Affirmations.

NIETZSCHE ON ATHEISM, PESSIMISM, SCHOPENHAUER

Translated by Thomas Common.

The Subjugation of a Shadow.

When Buddha was dead his shadow still continued to be seen for centuries afterwards in a cave, an immense frightful shadow. God is dead; but, as the human race is constituted there will perhaps continue to be caves for millenniums in which his shadow will be seen. And we—we have still to get the better of his shadow.

—*The Gay Science.*

The Progress of Freedom of Spirit.

One cannot better illustrate the difference between the earlier and the present freedom of spirit than by recollecting the saying which required all the intrepidity of the past century to recognise and express it, which however, when measured by the insight of the present day, sinks to an involuntary naiveté; I mean the saying of Voltaire: *Croyez-moi, mon ami, erreur aussi a son mérite.*"*

—*Miscellaneous Opinions.*

Schopenhauer.

It would be a question whether Schopenhauer with his Pessimism, i.e., the problem of the worth of existence, was necessarily only a German. I think not. The event after which this problem was to be expected with certainty, so that an astronomer of the soul could have calculated the day and hour for it—the decline of the

* "Believe me, my friend, error also has its merits." [ed.]

belief in the Christian God, the victory of scientific atheism—was a collective European event in which all races are supposed to have had their share of service and honour... Schopenhauer was the first avowed and inflexible atheist we Germans have had ; his hostility to Hegel had its ultimate motive here. The non-divinity of existence was regarded by him as something given, tangible, indiscussible ; he always lost his philosophical composure and got into a passion when he saw anyone hesitate and make circumlocutions here. It is at this point that his thorough uprightness of character comes in; unconditional honest atheism is precisely the prerequisite of his raising the problem, as a final and hard-won victory of the European conscience, as the most portentous act of two thousand years discipline to truth, which at the conclusion, no longer tolerates the lie of the belief in God. When we have thrust away from us the Christian Interpretation of things and have condemned its significance as spurious courage, we are immediately confronted in a striking manner with the Schopenhauerian question: Has existence then a significance at all? the question which will require a couple of centuries even to be completely heard in all its profundity. That which Schopenhauer himself answered with regard to this question was—forgive me for saying so—somewhat premature, somewhat juvenile, only a compromise, a persistence in and adhesion to the very same Christian-ascetic moral perspectives the belief in which had got warning to quit along with the belief in God. But he raised the question—as a good European, as we have said, and not as a German.

—*The Gay Science.*

The Sea Again Lies Open Before Us.

The greatest modern event—that "God is dead," that the belief in the Christian God has become unworthy of belief—has now begun to cast its first shadows over Europe. To the few at least, whose eye, whose suspecting glance is strong enough and subtle enough for the spectacle, a sun seems to have set to them, some old profound truth seems to have changed into doubt; our ancient world must daily seem to them older, stranger, more unreliable, more casual. In the main, however, we may say that the event itself is far too great, too much beyond the power of apprehension of many people for even the report of it to have reached them, much less for them to know what has really taken place thereby—and what must all collapse, after this belief has been undermined, by being built upon it, by being buttressed by it, by being engrafted into it: for example our entire European morality. The prolonged excess and continuation of, demolition, destruction, ruin and overthrow which is now impending—who has yet understood it sufficiently to be obliged to stand up as the teacher and herald of such a tremendously frightful inference, as the prophet of such an o'ershadowing, of such a solar eclipse as has probably never happened on earth before? Even we, the born riddle-readers, who, as it were, wait on the mountains, posted between to-day and to-morrow, engirt* by the contradiction between to-day and to-morrow, we firstlings and premature births of the coming century, to whom especially the shadows which must forthwith envelop Europe should already have come in sight—how is it that even we, without genuine sympathy for this o'ershadowing, contemplate its advent without personal solicitude or fear? Are we still perhaps too much under the influence of this event—and its immediate influence for us is the reverse of what could have been expected, not at all sad and depressing, but rather like a new and difficultly describable variety of light, happiness, alleviation, enlivenment, encouragement and rosy dawn? In fact, we philosophers and "free spirits" feel ourselves irradiated as by a new rosy dawn by the report that "the old God is dead;" our hearts thereby overflow with gratitude, astonishment, presentiment and expectation—at last

* *Engirt* means to surround or encircle. [ed.]

the horizon seems once more unobstructed, granting even that it is not bright; our ships can at last start on their voyage once more in face of every danger; every risk is again permitted to the knowing one; the sea, our sea, again lies open before us; perhaps there was never such an "open sea."

—The Gay Science.

Optimism and Pessimism Both Obsolete.

Away with the wearisomely hackneyed terms Optimism and Pessimism! For there is daily less and less occasion to use them; it is only the babblers for whom they are still indispensable. For why in all the world should anybody be an optimist unless he has a God to defend who must have created the best of worlds if he be divine goodness and perfection? What thinking man is there, however, who still requires the hypothesis of a God? But neither is there any occasion for a pessimistic confession of faith, unless it is to person's interest to be vexed with the advocates of God, the theologians or the theologizing philosophers, and to assert strongly the counter allegation: that evil rules, that non-delight is greater than delight, that the world is a piece of bungling, the manifestation of an ill-will to life. But who concerns himself any longer about the theologians?—except the theologians. Apart from theology and its contentions, it is obvious that the world is neither good nor bad (to say nothing of best or worst), and that these conceptions "good" and "bad" have significance only in relation to man, indeed, perhaps even here they are not authorised in the manner in which they are ordinarily used: we must by all means rid ourselves alike of the reviling and glorifying mode of contemplating the world.

—Human, All-too-human.

DARWINISM IN SOCIOLOGY: *A Reply To Nietzsche's Critics.*

Every consistent system, in its ultimate analysis, is made up of a comparatively small number of principles. If each of these principles is firmly established, then the system stands as a whole; if only some of them are established, the system is partially true and perhaps partially false; and if all its principles are disproved, then the system is absolutely worthless. Instead, therefore, of examining seriatim all the objections—some of them very trivial—that are brought against Nietzsche's system, let us briefly examine its most important principles, and if we find these firmly established or self-evident, then most of the objections will vanish of their own accord in candid, truth-loving minds.

1. In so far as there is a moral end at all, the highest social excellence, strength and vigour, is the only end that can be justified. The denial of this principle involves the absurdity that an inferior degree of social excellence is preferable to a higher social condition.

2. Human beings are not equal. The fact is obvious to everyone who is not wilfully blind. Those, however, who wish to know the extent of the inequality and understand the matter fully in its scientific bearings, should consult Mr. Francis Galton's *Hereditary Genius,* and his other works on the subject.*

3. Individuals, healthy and well-constituted in mind and body, instinctively seek their further self-development, their higher physical and mental excellence, and the perpetuation of their type.

* Mr. Francis Galton's investigations of the subject of human inequality furnish a firm basis on which an anonymous German writer has recently built up a theory of "social aristocracy." in a very important book, entitled, "*Service of the People (Volksdienst) by a Social Aristocrat.*" The author's erthusiasm for the abolition of hereditary property reminds one of Henry George's enthusiasm for his panacea.

4. The highest excellence, the greatest strength and vigour of the social organism and of the human type, can only be attained by the further self-development of the physically and mentally superior individuals.

5. It is for the interest of the human species with a view to its further advancement, that the better class of individuals should have greater advantages than inferior individuals. We shall regard this principle as obvious until the time comes when agriculturists and horticulturists (much wiser men than ethiculturists), with a view to raising the best crops, give to inferior plants and weeds the same advantageous conditions of growth as the best plants. It is therefore absurd to advocate equality of opportunity, Semi-idiots should not have the advantage of a university education, and should not be admitted to the British Museum Library. And it is still more absurd to advocate, as many ethiculturists appear to do, that the inferior class should be allowed to breed like vermin, and that their spawn should be supported at the cost of the better classes.

6. The interests of superior and inferior individuals are necessarily antagonistic; there has been a continuous conflict between them, and the inferior class have now gained a temporary ascendancy. The struggle for existence is universal among the lower animals; it is therefore strange that the struggle should be regarded as something abnormal among human beings. The conflict in the human species is however disguised; it is waged not so much with carnal as with spiritual weapons. Paul himself confesses that it is so; and the work which Paul performed in the world is the most important of all studies for the Darwinian. Paul may be said to have patented the most effective imposture ever devised for giving advantage to the inferior class in the struggle for existence—namely, the system for "saving sinners"; and by so doing he has perhaps done more harm in the world than all the other scourges. of humanity taken together. To be sure the salva-

tion promised is in another world, but the real purpose of the system—to save unworthy individuals in the present world—is thereby the better concealed. Christianity is the artful device by means of which 1. the slave class has successfully accomplished a revolt in half the world. We are greatly indebted to Dr. Alfred Russell Wallace for being the first to show the immense role which mimicry (the falsehood, imposture and hypocrisy of the lower animals) plays in nature; it would surely be surprising if something of a similar kind did not present itself among human beings. All the devices of ascetic priests are of the nature of mimicry, they are devices for enabling inferior beings to maintain themselves in the hard struggle for existence in which they cannot compete on equal terms with the strong and healthy. Christianity is the ascetic religion par excellence; it is such an extraordinarily perfect system of mimicry and imposture, especially in its ethical aspects, that it is no wonder that it imposed on the most intelligent men in past ages, and held the world in bondage for nearly 2000 years. When falsehood plays such an immense role in nature, he who acts on the maxim "Truth at all costs," will soon find by bitter experience that "honesty is the worst policy" in dealing with deceitful and dishonest men who have no regard for the welfare of the human race.

7. Owing to the breaking up of the old social groups incidental to new modes of living, a considerable maladjustment of social conditions has taken place in historic times, and socialism and commercialism being both unsatisfactory, mankind is now in quest of a new system of organization, under which advantages will once more be reaped approximately proportionate to natural ability. Some 2500 years ago the social conditions under which human beings lived began to alter considerably in the more civilized portions of the world, owing especially to the extension of commerce (which followed the increased use of iron) and the introduction of money. Under the commercial and financial system

with its substitution of gold for merit, advantages no longer accrue so approximately in proportion to natural ability, as under a non-monetary system which obliges every one to stand on his own merits. (Those who object to the word merit may put natural capacity in its place). Theognis, the Greek poet,* pointed out at a very early date the social evils which resulted from the new order of things; the maladjustment, however, has tended rather to increase than diminish in the course of ages. Mankind has consequently been groping about for two and a half millenniums for a new social system under which to live. This mal-adjustment gave the special opportunity for Christianity to spring up, which caused the revolt of the slaves by its socialistic and ultra-socialistic teaching. But socialism, Christian or non-Christian, can never be the basis of a sound system of society. The commercial system, notwithstanding the loud assurances of professional political economists and the editors of commercial newspapers, is equally far from being the best system for the distribution of social advantages. Though still inheriting some of the instincts of the heroic age, we live at present for the most part under an anarchical, make-shift system, a hybrid growth of commercialism and Christian socialism, under which advantages are distributed largely at hap-hazard, and not necessarily to the deserving, as they would be under the ideal social system. We must, however, find such a system; we must find men who can determine the merits and demerits, the valuable and the non-valuable qualities of their fellow-men, and who can reconstitute society on a new basis of genuine worth. From Nietzsche's point of view. therefore, which regards commercialism as an altogether imperfect system, the special question of rent and interest does not come up for discussion. I'm king rent and interest, however, as facts which exist at present, we should look at them with reference to the moral end

* Nietzsche was greatly influenced by the writings of Theognis; and Darwin also recognised their importance by quoting a passage from them on the deteriorating effect of money, in his *Descent of Man*.

we have in view—in so far as they are a hindrance to its attainment, we should try to counteract their evil influence.

Considering societies as organisms, and re-examining the subject according to analogy, we reach much the same results. Individuals are not analogous to the members of a physical organism, they are merely analogous to the cells, as Haeckel, Weismann, Roux, and others have shown. The individual cell, therefore, even in the most important organs, is of so comparatively small account, that, reasoning from analogy, we might conclude that not only the lack of equal advantages among certain human beings is in no way injurious to the social organism, but even their very extinction is a matter of indifference, especially if provision is made for others to take their place. Analogy, in fact, teaches us much more. Whole organs or groups of cells are no longer nourished when they are no longer needed, and are consequently lost (e.g., the four toes of the horse, the hind limbs of the whale, etc.); we should therefore expect that whole groups of individuals will be eliminated from the social organism, when they no longer serve a useful purpose. Further, there is not equality of opportunity in the cells of a physical organism; the cells that compose our little toes, for example, have not the advantage of the careful protection which the cells of the brain and spinal cord possess; consequently we may conclude that individuals destined to regulate society should have better opportunities than those who are likely to be comparatively worthless. It has also been shown by Roux that a struggle for existence goes on among the cells, and in all the parts of an organism; consequently we may expect that conflicts will take place among individuals and classes composing the same society. Human societies, however, are only analogous to low physical organisms; they are therefore able to exist under a variety of forms, and under favourable conditions many awkward and ill-constituted social organisms may continue to live. Analogy thus confirms the conclusions previously arrived at.

—*Thomas Common*

THE LAND OF THE ALTRUISTS

A Parable for the Infant Class.

If you start from the South Pole and sail due north, you will come to a wonderful country inhabited by the people called Altruists. They are called so because they prefer other people's happiness to their own.

They are a very industrious, hard-working, uncomplaining people, forever toiling from daylight till dark, making all kinds of useful and luxurious things; yet so unwilling are they to enjoy the fruits of their labour, so anxious for somebody else to be happy at their expense, that they have made this very ingenious and complete arrangement to secure that result.

They have ordained that everybody who has produced a thousand dollars worth of goods shall receive from the rest of the community sixty dollars a year; he who has made or obtained in any way ten thousand dollars worth shall receive six hundred dollars a year; and so on in proportion.

Now, it is easily seen that, as the people to whom these stipends are paid are at liberty to go on working and making enough to live on, they are able to lay by the amounts paid to them by the community. After a while these amounts become so large that they need not work at all, for all the rest of the Altruist community are pledged to support them, their children, grandchildren and great grandchildren, not only till death, but forever.

Such sweet and unselfish dispositions have these Altruists.

There are getting to be a good many of these people who are supported by the Altruists.

Two or three million at a guess in every twenty or thirty million families do not work, but are paid because they have so much already. They are getting very bossy, too, these stipendiaries of the workers, and begin to hold themselves very loftily, and despise the unselfish workers as dirty, ignorant, low creatures, unmindful of the fact that it is only because the workers are Altruists that they enjoy providing luxuries for others-rather than for themselves.

It is getting to be rather hard scratching, too, for the workers, Altruists though they be, who enjoy hunger and suffering; for to the objects of their care, the supported class, they have given, not only all the houses and furniture, and all but a little of the butter and meat and bread, but the very land itself, so that now, when the Altruist workers want to work still harder and to cultivate more land to support the rapidly-growing numbers of the Aristocrats, they find themselves forbidden by these very Aristocrats to use the land which they have given them.

Clearly a catastrophe must occur. Although the Altruists enjoy starving as long as they have the pleasure of seeing the Aristocrats, as they call those whom they support, have plenty, there is a physical limit to the process of starvation, and, when the Altruists begin to diminish in number, the Aristocrats must also dwindle.

What the outcome will be no man can prophesy—a relapse into slavery at least, which the Altruists would no doubt enjoy even more than their present arrangements; but there is a chance that their natures may change: they may become Egoists, and no longer take pleasure in giving to those who give nothing in return. Then there will be no Aristocrats, and everybody who is not an Altruist will have a much better time.

—John Beverley Robinson

WHY WOMEN NEED EGOISM

WOMEN have become more degenerated through altruism than men on account of their different conception of the meaning of altruism. Although the creed of the male altruist professedly is "to make others happy first," he insists upon it that his food is always properly cooked, his house and children must be clean, his wife is expected to submit to his marital rights, etc., etc. A male altruist has drawn up a set of laws, called by him marital duties, legalized by himself, which secure his comfort and ease. These duties must be fulfilled by the wife at all cost, no matter whether she is made unhappy or loses her health by them. The wife through her lack of time to think for herself believes this set of household laws or duties must be strictly obeyed in order to be a true woman. The consequence is the noticeable ugliness and bad health of female married altruists. Their habit of ceaseless giving or slaving makes them a disgrace to altruism. If it were a virtue to give profusely like the sun, as the Bible teaches, to give would make the giver more and more beautiful. If a "virtue" degenerates physically and mentally, it is a vice which should be shunned.

Where is salvation found for woman or is she destined to remain a contemptible slave? Disappointed altruists who desire to be healthy, beautiful, happy and wise will find in egoism their only salvation, because it teaches self-knowledge. Woman will learn to get hold of herself, to be her own guide. When she becomes clear-sighted through a rational way of living, she will herself discern where her duties lie. The duties of an egoistic woman lie in the same direction as those of an egoistic man, namely, first to make herself happy and secondly to make others happy. No egoistic woman will give a gift unless she has received one of equal value. She will make no one happy unless she is made happy likewise. This just and wise doctrine will act as a beautifier on women of all ages. The young will be made more beautiful and attractive and those advanced in years will be rejuvenated by it.

To an ambitious woman egoism offers a special inducement, because the knowledge how best to supply the needs of her body will rapidly develop her already great intuitive powers, in consequence of which she will be able to outwit any intellectual giant of a blunted psychic nature.

—Fraulein Lepper

APPRECIATION OF STIRNER

(From Max Stirner, sein Leben and sein Werk*)*
Translated by Thomas Common.

The significance of "The Sole One"* is still, as it was fifty years ago, divined and felt rather than known. How could it be otherwise in times when, in fact, everything totters to which we have hitherto clung, when we are zealously striving to replace the old estimates of worth by new ones, when the old stale wine is being again and again poured into new bottles instead of being poured away, and when we are still so little convinced of the absolute worthlessness of most of the estimates of worth!

We are a generation living betwixt night and day. Half awakened, we still rub our somnolent eyes, and are afraid to look into the light.

We cannot separate ourselves from the old abodes of our ideas, although they collapse over our heads; we are too cowardly to forsake the old home and commit ourselves to the sea of self-consciousness that can alone bear us to the other shore; we have not yet any genuine confidence in the future, although (or rather because) we have no longer confidence in ourselves.

We no longer believe in God; assuredly it is so. We have become atheists, but we have remained "pious people." We no longer pray in presence of the church bogey; we kneel before the sanctuaries of our heart.

We still get into estatic states as formerly, and the wretchedness of our awakening is the same. Only we awake more frequently, and our condition is that of reeling betwixt intoxication and doubt; it is no longer the holy, eternal ecstacy of the first "true" Christians.

---

* Referring here to Stirner's book *The Ego and Its Own* by an alternate translation of the title. [ed.]

Then this man comes amongst us.

He does not come with the condescension of the priest—he is not in the service of God, or of any idea whatsoever ; nor with the fussiness of the teacher—he leaves us to believe or reject what he says ; nor with the anxiety of the physician—he lets us live or die, for he knows that our fancy is our disease. Nor does he come like the philosopher who tries to catch us in the net of a new system of speculation. He despises the philosopher's language, the hideous, obscure, and unintelligible language, used as a privilege by those who only want to talk among themselves; he makes for himself a language of his own, for he knows that all knowledge can be intelligible when it wants to be intelligible.

He does not speak of us; he hardly even speaks to us.

He speaks of himself, and always of himself only ; and we see how this ego of his strips itself of one fetter after another, until it stands free and unconquerable, in proud self-splendour, as its own master, the last on the field which it has finally won.

It is nothing more nor less than the declaration of the sovereignty of the individual, his incomparability and his uniqueness, that Stirner announces. Hitherto one had only spoken of his rights and duties, and where they begin and end; Stirner, however, declares that we are exempt from the latter, and have control over the former. We must make our choice. And since we cannot go back into the night, we must enter into the day.

For we know now that we are all of us egoists. When we survey our actions, we see that some of them have carried us further, much further, than our consciousness wishes to acknowledge, while others have got us entangled in discords quite incapable of being harmonised. Henceforth it will be in vain for us any longer to attempt to deceive ourselves and others concerning the motives of our conduct. Now that we have acknowledged them, what else remains for us but to accomodate ourselves to them?

The result will teach us what we have to thank Stirner for,

if the example of those who have so lived their life has not yet shown it to us.

It is our final acknowledgment. Let us no longer stand up against it.

For verily, not too early does the day dawn, after this all-too-long night.

He has raised the bowed head, and put a sword into the languid hand. He has removed our faith and given us certainty.

He has again reminded us of our true interests, of our profane, personal particular-interests, and shown us that it is precisely their pursuit, and not sacrificing ourselves to ideal, sacred and external interests, to the interests of all, that brings back the happiness to life, which we seem to have lost.

Since he has dissected the state of the politician, the society of the socialist and the humanity of the humanist, and has made it obvious that they are limitations to our individuality, he has given the death-blow to all authority—at the same time destroying the majority's and collective body's sovereign will and privilege—and in place of the citizen, the worker, the man, comes the ego, in place of the incorporeal annihilator, the real creator!

But not that only. Since he devotes the other part of his work to the most thorough investigation of the conditions under which alone the ego is able to develop itself to its uniqueness, he exhibits it to us in its power, its intercourse, and its self-enjoyment–the medium of its force and its final victory.

And in place of our weary, sore-tortured, self-tormenting race, comes the proud, free race of the "sole ones," to which the future belongs.

He did what he has done for himself, because it was a pleasure to him.

He demands no thanks, and we owe him nothing.

He has only reminded us of our indebtedness to ourselves!—

That is what he has done; how he has done it is not less worthy of admiration.

If originality and force are signs of true genius, Max Stirner was a genius of the first rank. He sees the world and men entirely with his own eyes, and everything stands before him in the clearest light of actuality. Nothing can perturb or deceive his penetrating gaze ; neither the night of the past, nor the crowd of desires of his own age. His is an absolutely original work, and there is none that could have been written with more impartiality and freedom from prejudice than *The Sole One and His Prerogative.* There is nothing, absolutely nothing, which Stirner accepts as established and given, unless it be his own ego. Nothing bewilders him, confuses him, or imposes on him a priori. He thus appears as the genuine child of that critical age, only so infinitely in advance of it, that he begins where the others leave off. This impartiality gives to his words that self-intelligible assurance which so bewilders one person and acts so triumphantly on another.

The logic of this thinker is also incomparable. The rigid consistency of his conclusions does not shrink from any, not even from the ultimate consequences. He does not leave it to the reader to extend his thoughts to the limit of their sphere, he does it himself.

Conceptions which hitherto appeared unimpugnable, he decomposes one after another, and lets them crumble to dust.

It is not with the outer form of the Christian conception of things, of the rotten, crumbling church of the present day that this battle has to do, but with that spirit which, in ever new forms, continually constructs new strongholds of absolutism, the spirit of Christianity which, like a gloomy vapour, hangs over the past.

It is Stirner's achievement to have divested this spirit of its sanctity, to have unmasked it as the unsubstantial ghost of our imagination. While the most radical thinkers of his age Strauss, Feuerbach and Bauer merely groped with timorous criticism at the conceptions of sanctity, he decomposed them, and allowed them to crumble away.

He vanquishes Christianity in its ultimate consequences. It is annihilated. It lies behind us with the millennium of its humiliation, the smut of its fraternity, the innumerable horrors with which it has stained the page of history, with its falsehood, with its repudiation of all pride, of all individuality, of all genuine pleasure and beauty; and although it still prevails among us in its final effects, Stirner has nevertheless removed it from us as a curse!

He stands on the boundary-line between two worlds, and a new epoch in the life of the human race begins with him—the epoch of freedom.

As yet we have not found any better name for it than that of anarchy: the order determined by reciprocal interest, instead of the lack of order under the sway of power which has hitherto prevailed; the exclusive sovereignty of the individual over his personality, instead of his subjection; his responsibility for his own actions, instead of his tutelage—in short, his uniqueness.—For it is on the foundation of the Christian view of things that the supports of all those conceptions rest which uphold the sway of power; when Stirner has withdrawn the ground from under them, they must fall, and with them falls that which they have supported.

So violent will be this bloodless and proportionally rapid-and-sure revolution of all the relations of life, that his immortal book will one day be compared only with the Bible in its wide bearings.

And as this holy book stands at the commencement of the Christian era to carry its devastating effects for two thousand years into almost the remotest corners of the inhabited world, so does the unholy book of the first self conscious egoist stand at the entrance to the new age, under the first sign of which we live, to exercise as blessed an influence as that of the "book of books" was pernicious.

And if we would once more say what it is, how could we do it better than in its author's own words? It is this: "A violent, reckless, shameless, conscienceless, presumptuous—crime" perpetrated on the sanctity of all authority! And, hailing with joyous shouts the outburst of the purifying, emancipating storm conjured up by him, we ask with Max Stirner: "Do not the thunders roll in the distance, and dost thou not see how the heavens are ominously silent and becoming obscure?"

-John Henry Mackay

THAT BLESSED WORD ALTRUISM

I may have too much prejudice against this blessed word Altruism, but there is perhaps reason for it. The Altruists (genuine brand) I have met have been, as a rule, so infernally theoretical. An instance: when at college I knew a lovely youth who was always chanting the praises of Altruism. One day he read a little essay, "The girl that nobody would dance with," which painted such a desolate picture of this girl, sitting through a ball without an invitation to a single whirl, that I was compelled to weep. The essayist exhorted the rest of the students to look after this girl at our next ball, and ask her to dance early and often—in fact, I think he wanted to get her engaged through the whole evening, in order to avoid any spectacle that might have marred his enjoyment with the more popular girls. "Think," said the enthusiastic Altruist, "of the great pleasure you give the poor girl, so long neglected and spurned of men!" It was an unprincipled thing to do, but I decided to keep my eye on this Altruist, and I learned much more from his eloquent example than I did from his eloquent exhortation. Did he dance with "Patience on a Monument"—did he marry her? Alas! no. He married the most voluptuous maid that he knew; and I at once inferred that his nature was surcharged with a deep vein of poesy or liesy, and I considered myself "onto the game."

Another and a sadder case of Altruism in theory:—Once I found myself in St. Louis worse of than John the Baptist—not even one cent ahead. My conscience would not permit me to think of stealing—while so many policemen were about—and it began to look anything but "salubrious" for one of Nature's noblemen, as I had once been called by a fellow-student who borrowed five dollars from me the next day. In this state of complete spiritual and financial collapse, while wandering (aimlessly, as I thought, butt providentially, as the event proved) along 5th Street, in St. Louis, I saw the sign—

OFFICE OF THE "ALTRUIST."

Paul's light at Damascus was a farthing candle compared with the rainbow I saw above the blessed word. I spelled the word backwards and forwards. I took out a *Webster's Pocket Dictionary*, which I had sold roastin' ears to buy, in order to make sure that I understood the term. (Alas, there are so many things in heaven and earth that are not dreamed of in your dictionary, Master Noah!). I was afraid that, like Aeschylus, I would die of joy, or else, like Otway, kill myself by overeating. I conjured up repasts at all the leading hotels; and never dreamed that I would be asked to anything less than the Lindell or the Southern Hotels. At the very least, here was an open sesame to a picnic of interminable lunch counters. I was convinced, for the thousandth time, that I, too, was a man of destiny, and that the same power which had protected other great men in ages past was now miraculously exerted in my behalf, directing me to the office of the "Altruist." I wonder if the Editor of the "Altruist" still remembers my advent. I often think of him and his little printing-press (one of the kind alluded to by Bill Nye, "It would really have made a better cider press—it was too earnest in making an impression"); and often I wish we might meet again in a happier world—one that does not have to be saved every month or so. Well, to cut a long story amidships, the editor was as "hard-up" financially, if not spiritually, as myself; and, if it had not been for a dear German friend who ran an Apostle's lunch counter around the corner, and who was in a position to rescue the perishing practically, there would have been two more altruists that night seeking in supperless exaltation the sympathy of the stars.

—John Erwin McCall

AESCHYLUS AT MARATHON
Are we Saved by Love or by Hate?

Once for all, let us clear our minds of cant. Let us rise to the noble honesty of the Greek attitude which faithfully reflected the sanity and the sanctity of Hate. Can we find a more faithful or more inspiring embodiment of this noble pagan position than in the beautiful, hate-breathing epitaph which Aeschylus wrote for himself? Here it is:

> Athenian Aeschylus, Euphorion's son,
> Buried in Geta's fields these lines declare;
> His deeds are registered at Marathon,
> Known to the deep-haired Mede, who met him there.

We wish to offer a few observations on one phase of the opinions elicited by our Symposium. We desire to reason in the most patient manner possible with the most misguided beings who have ever obstructed human progress, we mean the well-meaning but deluded Tolstoyans. The Tolstoyans tell us that Love is the only remedy for social misery. When the Tolstoyan stands before the victim of oppression and outrage, it is thus that he addresses the suffering man: "It is true that the oppressor has robbed you not only of the chance of a decent existence, but has condemned your wife to life-long starvation and your daughters to prostitution; nevertheless you are still more blessed than your murderer and exploiter because you have done no evil; and you must still love the instrument of your afflictions. You are far more prosperous than he is, although you are in this sorry light, because you have the approval of your conscience even while you are starving, and if you continue to love.him till you starve to death, you will be numbered with the saints: in glory everlasting." When the Tolstoyans, mock our miseries with such precious consolations (for I have but reduced their doctrines to their logical, conclusion) I am compelled to say to them that it is such unutterable imbecilities as these which drive us to despair of humanity. Against such stupidities omnipotence itself must contend in vain. While these insanities meet us at every turn, progress is all but impossible—our perpetual damnation is the only thing of which we can be certain. Tolstoyans tell us that social syncope exists because men do not love enough. We believe in the antithesis of this statement—we believe that, so far as it is not inherent in human nature, social misery exists because men do not hate enough. Love rarely inspires thought, and indeed its apostles tell us that with love no thought is necessary, that love is a substitute for thought. No apostle of Hate has ever talked such nonsense—it has never been alleged that Hate is a substitute for thought, but we have abundant proof that profound hatred has inspired some of the most impressive streams of thought, some of the most powerful intellects of all time. Karl Marx, quoting George Sand, declares "On the eve bleach general reconstruction of society, the last word, of social science will ever be

> "Combat or death; bloody struggle or extinction,
> "It is thus that the question is irresistibly put."

H. M. Hyndman wrote: "It is precisely the hatred and disgust I feel for the misery, degradation and physical deterioration around me which had more influence in making and keeping me a Social Democrat than anything else." William Morris, writing on "How I Became a Socialist," says: "To sum up then, the study of history and the love and practice of art forced me into a hatred of [the existing] civilisation."

In a world whose characteristics were prevailingly "lovely," love would best become a man, but in a world whose leading features are to the last degree unlovely, hypocritical and hateful, hate is the only sentiment an honest man can entertain. Hence it follows that in this predominantly hateful world, men of hate leave their impress on every page of history, while men of love, with their pale and ineffectual negations, have their day and cease to be. Hannibal, Napoleon, Nelson, Danton, Mirabea, Byron, Attilla, Morris, Marx, Proudhon— these names stand as sublime coefficients of vast streams of Hate.

What are the greatest events in modern history, its most inspiring episodes? They are: Tell, Hampden, Milton, or Cromwell, hating and resisting the tyrant to the death; Nelson's exploits with his middies, inspired to glorious deeds by their hatred of Napoleon and the French; Napoleon's achievements with his Grenadiers, whose inspiring motive was hatred, first, of their own aristocracy, and then of the enemies of the Eagle Paris razing the Bastille, France liquidating eight centuries of misery, Patrick Henry exclaiming "If this be treason make the most of it"; the embattled farmers firing at the Bridge of Concord (Discord) rather the shot heard round the world, the shot of which Emerson wrote: "Their deed of blood all mankind praise, Even the serene reason says, It was well done"; Victor Hugo pouring the vials of his hate upon Napoleon the Little. These are the inspirations of Hate and they are among the noblest chapters of human history.

The great Haters are the great Lovers. Love Which does not hate the hateful as profoundly as it loves the lovely is mere hyprocrisy. Let us seriously ask the question, Do the predominant characteristics of the present age attract or repel an honest soul—in-other words, is our present age hateful or the reverse? We ought to base our answer upon the opinions of those whose honesty, capacity and experience entitle them to pronounce judgment on this issue. We present a series of such opinions in the article VIA HELLOROSA (see pg. 111). Those whom we have quoted are not journalists, statesmen, or Doctors of Divinity—but perhaps are not less trustworthy on that account. We believe that a consideration of the unbought opinions of Hugo, Heine, Lemennais, etc., will convince any free mind that the world has now reached the most murderous, most hypocritical, most hateful stage of social evolution known to history. Shall we love or shall We hate this horrible epoch which has been cursed by the united execrations of Heine, Hugo, Marx, Proudhon, Nietzsche, Shaw, Tucker, Morris, Redbeard, and Wallace? Surely, not to hate in the profoundest possible manner, such an era, which presents an apotheosis of legitimised assassination and worshipped hypocrisy, is to confess oneself a defender of assassins and a devotee of prostitutes and pirates. When one considers the systematic slaughter of the young and helpless, when one ponders the malign influence of our boasted institutions upon thousands of young men and young women, robbing them, as it does, of their unreturning May time and condemning them to lives of unescapable ignorance, bitterness and vice, institutions which murder thousands to give to a few, luxuries as maleficent as the evils they rest upon, when one has circumnavigated this continent and sub-continent of misery, then one asks oneself the question, How can I sufficiently bate and curse this frightful epoch with which I am fatally contemporaneous?

Let us then, like Aeschylus of old, go forth to meet the Mede which threatens the self-realisation of the Free, with a spirit of Hate as unalterable as his own laws, and in a manner that he will be able to appreciate. If time permit, let us give our enemy a decent burial on the field of our vindication, and if time do not permit we shall leave the dead to bury their dead. But on our field of Marathon we shall erect, with due libations, a trophy of accomplished Hate and Love—of Love for ourselves and our own, of Hate for all that threatens us and ours.

—John Erwin McCall,
Founder of the Religion of Hate.

THE RELIGION OF EGOISM

A Prayer for more Bitterness.

BRETHREN, we must become more bitter. Bitterness is the best antidote to the Christian slave-pox which for two thousand years has poisoned our blood. Said Emerson (my faithful ally in this and many another matter) "The doctrine of hatred must be preached as the counteraction of the doctrine of love when that pules and whines." We are all pulers and whiners to-day—we are born such and rarely out-grow it. Bitterness is the only thing which can tear the bandage of Idealism from our eyes and enable us to see life as the old unseduced Greeks and Romans saw it. And when we can see life as the Greeks and Romans saw it, perhaps we will have no further use for bitterness and can then throw it away. When the poison of Idealism is extirpated, then, perhaps, will come to pass the saying of Zarathustra, "Growth in wisdom is measured by decrease in bitterness."

Blessed is the man who has felt the deepest and best of all bitternesses—the bitterness of one starving in the midst of plenty—and who is made a giant and a clairvoyant by that bitterness. Herein I have an advantage over Nietzsche, who unfortunately always knew where his next meal was coming from. If I, Erwin McCall, had not been for years to all intents and purposes a DAMNED TRAMP—with never an assured meal ahead—I would never have been saved. It was this (philosophic) blessing of ever imminent starvation which made me see life as it is—bared of all its hypocrisies—made me see that "He who feeds me governs me" or as Bacon said "Nations and wars go on their bellies." It is a good starvation which also starves the "Ideal." Thus the tramp who has brains will learn what it took Nietzsche years of fatal devotion to literature to ascertain. If Nietzsche had had a couple of weeks' tramping among friends and real Christians he would have learned in that time all that Montaigne, Chamfort and Co. could teach him, and the tree would have defied the lightning for another half-century.

The prospect of starvation may even save the soul of a millionaire—let us not be selfish with this last and best gift of the gods, starvation, but let us pass it round and redeem the rich from their intellectual poverty.

And then—and then—it must be said, although it will be misunderstood: only he who has been once thoroughly bitter can know how sweet love is. Man is fearfully and wonderfully made and truly our heaven and our hell are inseparably intertwined. Avaunt, logician, you have no antinomies like those of the human heart. This prayer for bitterness has relieved me immensely—if the mere aspira- tion for bitterness thus makes blessed, how ecstatic must be a deed of bitterness.

A Bible Not Borrowed from the Neighbors.

EMERSON the Egoist said "All laws are laughable but those which men make for themselves." It is time to say that all Bibles are to be rejected save that which we write for ourselves. The Bible of Jesus, of Goethe, of Heine, of Emerson, of Whitman, of Thoreau, of Nietzsche,—all these may help us somewhat but we must have pride enough to demand a Bible not borrowed from the neighbors. A slave may rest content with a Bible writ by another, the freeman must write his own. Vicarious suffering, vicarious salvation are out of date. We may weep over the sorrows of Jesus and Nietzsche, we may rejoice over their triumphs—but we are not saved till we weep over our own sorrows and rejoice in our own happiness, till we are deified by our own Calvary, till we can show our own Via Dolorosa, our own Gethsemane agony and exultation.

The Egoist learns to say:—"I, too, have a Divine Record—the

record of my innermost griefs, sorrows, temptations, triumphs, tears and rejoicings." We no longer accept salvation second-hand, we demand an original, an egoistic, salvation. Saved we are by love of self, pity for self, tears for our own incommunicable woe, but, last and best revelation, we are taught to strengthen and purify ourselves by laughing over our dire mistakes. Such laughter is the divinest emotion. Jove and the lions never weep, but often laugh. "The artist only reaches the last summit of his greatness when he learns how to laugh at himself"—he alone can go forward.

But some one says, Does the Religion of Egoism cure our sorrows as did the old Religion? We reply, What sorrows? Whose sorrows? The sorrows of a fool? To all such we say, The New Gospel is not milk for crying babes. We may add that the greatest injury you can do to a fool is to cure his sorrow—his only teacher. And the wise man will cure his own sorrows. After all, the New Religion deals generously enough with the sorrowing one. It makes each one of us the only God in the universe. What more do you want? And if a God cannot cure his own sorrows, the world will begin to doubt his divinity. We repeat what we learned in the cradle, that it is a shame not to have your own Bible and God in your own Ego's home, it is a shame to be obliged to borrow these from the neighbors. Moreover the founders of new Religions have always lived above the question of consolation—and every Egoist is the founder of a new Religion.

An Egoist's Confession of Faith in Himself.

FOR greater convenience in discerning and damning our enemies we have taken out a legal authority which permits us to divide all Egoists into two classes—philosophers and scoundrels. In our unwritten tract "Why I am an Altruist," by A. Skinflint, we exhibit this confession of the egoist-scoundrel: "Having made a cool million by as cool a steal, I straightway endowed ten chairs for the teaching of altruism. Never was I more sincere than in so doing, for, the more altruists, the more victims for me."

The best things are always the worst. Intemperance is only the abuse of the power of digestion. Unbridled lust is but love turned awry. Thus Egoism, the best thing in the world, may by abuse become murder, and scoundrelism of every sort. Every scoundrel is an Egoist but not every Egoist is a scoundrel.

By the egoist-philosopher (Hail to thee! death-dedicated apostle!) we mean the man who has the courage to proclaim the law of universal gravitation in ethics—that each ego is the centre towards which all things gravitate. He is the only man who wears his heart upon his sleeve for daws and even for men to peck at. I am sorry to say that he appears to be the only honest man in the world for he alone has found himself out and tells himself out. But he does more—he finds out those who think they are serving the heavenly ideal and he shows them they are fools, while the pseudo-altruist (egoist-scoundrel) says nothing but fattens on their foolishness.

It is a well-known fact that the preacher, whether of altruism or egoism, rarely practises what he preaches. In the *Clarion* Mr. A. M. Thompson gently chides us for devoting our "very conspicuous talents to the cause of advancing everybody's interests but" our own. "That's me all over"—in fact that is pre-eminently the egoist-philosopher. But every egoist-scoundrel must be a professed and professional altruist—every man who goes forth seeking whom he may devour must profess to be an altruist as the very condition of attracting victims to his net. But the man who avows himself an egoist scares away every possible victim from his net—or, more correctly, he throws away the net itself. Our language is not sufficiently expressive to enable us to state the paradoxes of our nature but the stern fact is that the egoist-philosopher is the only man who shows any real pity for men—the only man who shows them the only possible means of salvation. We egoist-philosophers are the only people who possess any real sympathy. Precisely because we do not prate of sympathy (the devil take this exception) do we possess the more. It is through the terrible calvary of our feelings (feelings too deep for thought) that we have fought our way to the egoistic philosophy of life—that invincible fortress defended by Epicurus on the one hand and the Stoics on the other. In combatting sympathy, we, like Nietzsche, combat the overcharged heart whose terrible inundations of sympathy would, if not ruthlessly restrained, swamp the free action of the intellect.

Be sure then of this—the man who devotes his days and nights and the money of all his dearest friends to the preaching of an egoistic philosophy, there-lay materially imperilling his awn chances in life, is necessarily nobler than the so-called altruist whose very creed is a sort of blackmail levied on the goodness and the goods of applauding fool-millions. Then the avowed Egoist and Atheist (shall we coin a word, Athegoist) who proclaims the true gospel of salvation, is not a knave though all the high-priced clerics and all the M.P.s and the whole gang of professional and endowed prostitutes declare him such; but, I repeat, he, as the only man who wears his heart upon his sleeve is the one honest man in the universe, the only man who has found himself out and told himself out. But the world with its usual supernatural and superasinine stupidity worships the scoundrel and keeps its obloquy for the honest philosopher. Such are the miracles of unreason which crown and culminate two thousand years of christian idiocy, such the result of feeding ourselves on babe's milk, stale for twenty centuries by the clock.

Verily, we egoist-philosophers, we "destroyers of false hopes, are the true Messiahs"*; we sacrifice ourselves for the sins of the past and for the happiness of future generations; we are the only genuine martyrs, for whom no subscriptions are raised, no civil list exists. In an age given over to the worship of altruism, the

---

* From Ragnar Redbeard's *Might is Right.* [ed.]

unmitigated egoist-philosopher must necessarily be a martyr. I mention Nietzsche in a madhouse and Stirner starved to death. But there are others.

The Calvary of Egoism.

EVEN the Egoist has his Calvary, but it is a home-made Calvary, just as the Egoist's Bible is home-made. It is of suicide I speak, of a death self-decreed and self-executed, not of a death forced on one by a mob of fools and fanatics. ("Natural death is a coward's death. We should desire a different kind of death—voluntary; conscious, not accidental or by surprise."—Nietzsche)

It is time for the Egoist to give to the world a new Stabat Mater. The egoist-suicide speaks from his Cross with a hitherto forbidden eloquence—he speaks these bitter truths which man has hitherto lacked the courage for uttering:

Mother, behold thy prattling babe,
Behold the Suicide thou hast made!

Yes, mother, thou art the cause of this suicide. Listen to me, listen to this voice from the grave: There was not a lie perfectly calculated to unfit me for life which you did not faithfully instil into me. You did your work most perfectly. You poisoned me from my earliest years by teaching to me as the very word of God and means of eternal salvation, every superstition and every delusion which could deliver me bound into the hands of all the Shylocks and all the Judases of earth. I spent the best years of my life believing the Bible and trying to live it—and here am I. I would prefer to entrust myself to the mercy of the Devil (if one existed) than to such a fool of a mother as you have been to me. Truly, mother, thou has been a benefactor to man. Thou madest me (too late) a philosopher and I must bless thee for that? (I would have truly blessed thee if thou hadst made me a philosopher in the cradle). Thou madest me a suicide and others will bless thee for that. Verily it is no small credit to thee that thou didst remove the curse and the curser thou didst create.

Will Christian journals please copy? And now, brethren, receive the benediction—"Here's to the health of the next one that dies." Thus endeth the fabrication for the first day.

—*Lord Erwin McCall*

15260303R00092

Printed in Great Britain
by Amazon